The Hidden Bible

The Hidden Bible

Michael Wood

Tubi Publishing, LLC

The Hidden Bible

Copyright © 2010 by Michael Wood

ISBN: 978-1-936565-00-9 (pbk)
ISBN: 978-1-936565-01-6 (hrc)
ISBN: 978-1-936565-02-3 (ebk)

Printed in the United States of America

Acknowledgments

To Osvaldo Jerez and Esteban Serrano, whose encouragement and support are appreciated more than words can possibly express.

A very special thanks to Jaime Alberto Castano.

And gratitude for David Compton, who helped to breathe life into my words.

Chapter 1

Robert turned the rented blue Lexus onto Maple Lane. "Almost there," he said with a smile.

Maria, the lone passenger in his car, looked down at the diamond ring on her left ring finger. "I can't wait for you to tell your mother that we're finally getting married."

The smile on Robert's face disappeared.

Maria noticed. "How's your mom been feeling lately?" she asked, placing her left hand gently upon Robert's thigh.

"I think she tries to hide her bad days from me. I'm really happy she's outlived her diagnosis, but I'm very concerned that the cancer has never been in remission."

Just then, Robert saw a neighbor walking alongside the quiet street. He slowed the car and rolled down the window. "Hi, Mrs. Johnson!" he hollered.

"Robert! It's so nice to see you," Mrs. Johnson shouted back.

Robert pulled alongside her.

A troubled look crossed her face. "I was just coming from your mother's house."

"Mom told me how you look after her every day. Thank you."

"I'm glad to do it. Your mom and I have grown so close over the years — especially since she joined the church. I just couldn't be happier that you have a week off college to come see her now."

Maria chimed in, grinning ear to ear, "And we have a very big surprise for her." She lifted her left hand, showing Mrs. Johnson the diamond ring.

Mrs. Johnson simply stood there, staring at Robert.

Robert remained silent for a moment, and then they said their good-byes and drove onto his mother's driveway.

Maria pointed to the bumper sticker on his mother's car as they pulled to a stop: *Warning: In case of Rapture, this car will be unmanned.*

Robert opened the car door for Maria, looked to the house and

1

sighed. Inside, a television was on at high volume.

¤ ¤ ¤

Robert carried the luggage in and escorted Maria to the spare bedroom, suggesting she freshen up while he checked on his mother.

After dropping off his own bag in his room, Robert headed to his mother's bedroom. The door was open, and he could see his mother resting in bed, watching television.

"Hi, honey, come in and give your mother a hug."

Robert walked over and held his mom.

On the television, a televangelist was thumping the pulpit, shouting into the microphone: "And Israel has become a nation once again, just like the Bible prophesied. And we all know what the next big event is — the Rapture! Jesus is coming soon to whisk his church up to heaven, and then the rest of the world will be left behind to face the Antichrist, the terrible Beast described in the book of Revelation. How awful it's going to be for those left behind! The Bible says this is going to be the most horrific time the world has ever known. Even Hitler's Holocaust will pale in comparison to the torments humanity is going to suffer after Jesus takes his church up to heaven. Can anyone doubt that the most important decision anyone can make in their lives is to be saved so they aren't left behind when Jesus comes?"

His mom's eyes were glued to the TV. The color drained from her face and a tear fell from her eye. "Honey, I'm just absolutely terrified I'm not going to be around to make sure you become Christian in time. I'm having constant nightmares of you missing the Rapture and I can't stand the thought of you having to face the terrible Beast of Revelation."

"But Mom, Maria's Christian. And I've recently started going to her church."

Through the pain on her face, Robert's mother could still manage a discernable frown. "You still don't understand," she said. "I used to think that all churches were fine, too, until Mrs. Johnson taught me how to be saved the Bible way. Only after I was saved did I learn that Pat Robertson, and the other godly men, teach that Maria's church — the Presbyterian Church — was established by the Antichrist himself.[1] The Devil created those churches to deceive people into believing they're Christians when they're not saved. I'm so afraid your feelings for her are going to keep you from making the Rapture."

Just then, Robert noticed that Maria was standing just outside the door. He knew she must have been waiting to hear Robert announce their engagement. He quickly stepped into the hallway.

"Maria!"

He saw tears streaming down her face and heard her gasping breaths, just before she went to her room and slammed the door closed behind her.

---

1   "You say you're supposed to be nice to the Episcopalians and the Presbyterians and the Methodists and this, that, and the other thing. Nonsense, I don't have to be nice to the spirit of the Antichrist."—Pat Robertson, The 700 Club, January 14, 1991

Chapter 2

About an hour later, Maria heard a knock on the door. "Come in," she answered.

Robert opened the door and went in. When he saw Maria's bloodshot eyes and tear-soaked pillow, he rushed over and wrapped his arms around her. "Honey, what's wrong?"

"I heard what your mom said about me," Maria answered.

"Oh my God, you heard our fight?" Robert gasped.

Maria shook her head. "No... But I heard your mom believes I go to a church run by the Antichrist, and she believes that your relationship with me is costing you your soul."

Robert remained silent.

Maria wiped the tear stains from her face. "Did you tell your mom about our engagement?"

Robert gulped. "No... We've been fighting about my feelings for you for the past hour."

Maria removed the ring from her left finger and put it in her pocket. "I'll give you all the time you need. Tell your mom at the moment you think is best."

"Thank you," Robert whispered.

¤ ¤ ¤

"May I help?" Maria asked later that evening, as Robert's mother began pulling pots and pans from the kitchen cupboards.

"Thank you, dear."

Robert offered to help, too, but they shooed him away. Sitting on a chair at the dining table, he watched warily as his fiancée and his mother began preparing dinner. They made it through an hour of chopping vegetables and cooking a pork roast without any drama. No one said anything controversial as they ate, though Robert thought several times that his mother was about to wander off safe subjects, before returning to talking about current events or the weather.

Robert cleared the dishes from the table. Maria insisted that she be allowed to clean up at the sink herself.

Robert's mom sipped coffee then turned to him and said, "My church is going to show a movie this evening. I think you and Maria might enjoy seeing it. I'll be fine here by myself."

"What's it about?"

"The end of the world. The movie shows what's going to happen after Jesus raptures the Christians up to heaven. It shows all the terrible things that the Beast of Revelation is going to do to those who are left behind."

Robert saw Maria give a warning look over her shoulder.

"Thanks, but I think I'll pass, Mom."

After a couple moments of silence, Robert's mother asked, "Maria, you're a senior like Robert, aren't you? What are your plans after graduation?"

Maria looked over at Robert.

Robert stared back at her for a moment. Then he took a deep breath and declared, "Actually, Maria and I have plans together after graduation." Robert motioned to Maria. "Honey, why don't you show her?"

Robert could see the surprise on Maria's face. But she cautiously reached into her pocket and pulled out the diamond ring.

The instant Robert's mother saw the ring, she slammed the dish she was holding onto the counter and shouted, "I'm so disappointed in you, Robert!" And without saying another word, she went to her bedroom and slammed the door.

The blood had drained from Maria's face. She dried her hands and slumped in a chair.

"I'm sorry," Robert said. "I thought about it, and I didn't want you to have to wait any longer. It's not fair."

After a few moments of silence, Maria took Robert's hand. "Tell you what. In the interest of reconciliation, why don't we go to that movie at your mother's church? Maybe that'll make her feel better."

"Are you kidding?"

"It's worth a try."

¤ ¤ ¤

The lights in the auditorium went down and the movie began in a dramatic fashion. The main character woke in the morning to find his wife missing. The negligee she was wearing the night before was still underneath the sheets next to him. When he turned on the television, he found that mass confusion had erupted around the world: the earth was filled with car crashes, people looking for missing loved ones, and all the babies in the world had disappeared. Then for the rest of the movie, tragedy after tragedy unfolded, especially after the Beast of Revelation appeared on the scene.

As the movie ended and the lights were turned on, Maria looked in Robert's direction. He was white as a ghost and shaking badly.

"What's wrong?" Maria mouthed to him, but he didn't respond.

The pastor started speaking. "My friends, you don't have to be left behind when Jesus comes. You don't have to face the Beast of Revelation. All you have to do is accept Jesus as your personal savior and you can avoid all the horrors this film has so graphically portrayed."

Soft moody organ music began to play as the preacher continued. "I invite you — no, I plead with you — to come down to this altar and be saved. It's the most important decision you will make in your lifetime."

Scores of people leapt from their seats, sobbing as they headed toward the altar.

"That's right, folks," the preacher said. "Come on down."

Maria turned to make a remark to Robert, only to find that he had already left his seat and was walking toward the altar, still shaking and looking very disturbed.

After watching Robert make it all the way to the altar and witnessing the preacher placing his hands onto his head, Maria decided to go outside and wait for him in the car.

Chapter 3

"Pastor, I'm confused," Robert said.

"Why, what's confusing you?"

"The film I just saw. I'm just blown away."

Robert sat in a comfortable armchair facing the pastor. It had been less than fifteen minutes since the end of the service, when the pastor had escorted Robert to his office. All the while, he had been in a daze, trying to make sense of what was going on. It was unlike anything that had happened to him in a church before.

Robert explained. "In my fiancée's church, they teach that one thing — and one thing only — determines the fate of our souls on Judgment Day: how much we helped other people while we were alive. Her pastor says that nothing else matters."

"So your fiancée's church teaches that people are saved from Hell by what they do — by their works," said the pastor, before grabbing a Bible that was lying on his desk. He opened it and pointed to a sentence, which had parts of it underlined. "Robert, why don't you read this sentence aloud?"

Robert read, "For by grace ye are saved by faith… *not by works,* lest any man should boast."[2]

The pastor nodded. "You see, Robert, the Bible is very clear in this matter. No one can make it to heaven by their efforts. And anyone who tries is in for a big surprise when Jesus raptures up those who received his salvation by faith."

"That sentence in the Bible is really clear," Robert said. "So then, why does my fiancée's church teach that salvation depends on how well we treat everyone around us?"

The pastor explained. "The answer is simple. Liberal churches don't believe in the Bible. I don't even know why they use it in their services. After all, the Bible says over and over again that salvation comes by only one way — *faith* in Jesus Christ." The pastor flipped

---

2 Ephesians 2:8-9

the pages of his Bible. He pointed to another underlined sentence and motioned for Robert to read it.

Robert read the words aloud. "God, who hath saved us, and called us with a holy calling, *not according to our works*, but according to his own purpose and grace."[3]

The pastor smiled. "You see how clear the Bible is on this matter? I can show you many more passages that say the same thing."

Robert swallowed hard. "No need. My mom's been telling me this for years. Now I see that she's been right all along. I hate that she's right about my fiancée's church. They really aren't a Christian church — just like mom always says. So if that's the case, can you show me how to be saved by faith?"

"There's nothing I'd rather do."

After Robert prayed the Prayer of Salvation, he felt a great physical and emotional release.

Then the pastor said, "Robert, while salvation is a gift by faith, we still believe in following all the teachings of the Bible, even when they are very difficult."

"Of course. And I want to follow the Bible, too."

The pastor paused for a moment then said in a very serious tone, "The Bible is very clear that a Christian should 'not be equally yoked with an unbeliever.'[4]"

"What are you trying to say?"

"I'm saying that you should give serious consideration about canceling your marriage to your fiancée."

"I'm not going to break up with her just because I became a Christian," Robert balked. "A real Christian."

"This command from the Bible is more for her sake than yours," the pastor continued.

Robert furrowed his brow. "What are you talking about?"

The pastor explained. "I want you to imagine that you go ahead and get married to Maria. And because you didn't take a stand, you're the only one that Jesus takes when he comes to rapture the church. And now, from the balcony of heaven, you have to watch Maria face the Beast of Revelation and all the horrible torments that follow. And remember, the Bible says that the moment she takes the number of

---

3 2 Timothy 1:9
4 2 Corinthians 6:14

the Beast — 666 — on her forehead or right-hand, there's no turning back."

Robert's mind raced to comprehend what he was hearing and tried to reconcile it with his newfound salvation.

The pastor paused for dramatic effect. "Do you love her enough to take a stand on her behalf?"

Chapter 4

Robert didn't say a word during the entire drive back to his mother's house. After he and Maria went inside, he faked a yawn. "It's late. Why don't we go to sleep and tell Mom we went to see the movie in the morning."

During the night, Robert had a startlingly vivid dream. In his dream, he was at the mall with his wife, Maria, and their newborn son. Suddenly, in the twinkling of an eye, Robert and his son were snatched up to heaven... Maria was left behind. Then he was shouting from heaven for Maria to accept Jesus before it was too late — but Maria couldn't hear him. Robert was beside himself when he saw Maria standing in line waiting to receive the mark of the Beast — 666 — on her forehead. He knew that the moment those numbers were engraved on her skin, the fate of her soul would be sealed forever. Unable to bear it any longer, Robert awoke from his dream, sweating and screaming, "Maria, no!"

¤ ¤ ¤

In the morning, Robert got out of bed and went to his mother's room straightaway. He was surprised to see the door still closed, as she was usually an early bird.

Robert knocked on the door, but there was no response. "Mom!" he called out. "It's me. Can I come in?" There was still no response.

Robert got a terrible pang in his gut. He reached for the doorknob and gave it a turn. Slowly, he opened the door. In the half-light, he could see his mother lying in bed, her eyes peacefully closed, her hands clasped over her chest. "Mom," Robert said quietly, one last time, before walking over. Again... nothing.

Robert pulled the curtains back and saw the dark, waxy skin-tone of his mother's face. He placed his hand on her cheek. As he felt the cold skin, he realized the day he was dreading had finally arrived. Robert bent over, cradled his mother's frail body, and cried. Robert recalled the last words she had said to him, "I'm so disappointed in you, Robert," and cemented his resolve to deal with his relationship with Maria.

Stroking his mother's hair, he said aloud, "I will be a good Christian. I will make you proud."

¤ ¤ ¤

"Thank you so much for being here," Robert told Maria, as they sat at his mother's kitchen table after the funeral home had left with his mother's body. "I'm so grateful to have you in my life."

Robert's mother had no siblings and neither did he, so he had complete responsibility for making all the arrangements. Maria had been involved in organizing her grandmother's funeral only two years earlier, so she knew the ropes. They picked out the simple oak casket together from the funeral home's showroom and Maria helped Robert find his mother's will, which made reference to a plot she had bought years earlier in the large city cemetery. Maria ordered a wreath of flowers and arranged for the death announcement in the newspaper.

The pastor at her church suggested a memorial service in the church's small chapel, which was attended by several women from his mother's Sunday School class. As she had been sick for such a long time, his mother had lost touch with many of her old friends and Robert didn't have time to track them down. There was a brief graveside service, a bleak affair on a gloomy day.

"It's okay to cry," Maria told him, as the service concluded.

Robert squeezed her hand hard, fighting back a torrent of tears. But it wasn't just the sorrow of his mother's death that saddened him. He was thinking ahead to the possibility of a life without Maria by his side.

Chapter 5

Robert tried to speak, but his voice was shaking too hard. He had rehearsed in his head what he was going to say to Maria the whole drive back to the university campus. Now they were parked in her sorority house parking lot. Robert prayed for the courage to get it out without putting it off another minute.

"What is it?" Maria asked. "It's okay. I know you're still very upset about your mother."

He gripped the steering wheel hard to steady his hands. Finally, he was able to calm down enough to turn and look her directly in the eye. "There's something very important we need to talk about." Robert took a deep breath, then said, "Babe, I love you so much and I just can't bear the thought of you being left behind when Jesus returns. I'm even having awful nightmares about it."

Maria sighed in relief. "Is that all?" She gave a little laugh. "Relax, honey! I don't even believe in that Rapture stuff. And besides, I'm a Christian, so you don't have anything to worry about!"

Robert took her hand. "I know you think you're Christian. But the Bible says that only those who receive Jesus' atonement by faith are the ones who are saved."

Maria grimaced. "Oh, give me a break. I'm doing my best to be patient with all the garbage you were taught at your mother's church."

"Garbage?" Robert said, suddenly raising his voice. "That's what you call the teachings of the Bible?"

"Well, I don't know a lot about the Bible, but what you're saying makes no sense at all. It actually sounds backwards. Fundamentalist churches like your mother's spend so much time trying to get people to 'get their souls right with God by faith,' as if that's somehow more important than meeting the humanitarian needs of those suffering in this world."

Robert hardened. "The more you talk, the more I realize that my mother and her pastor are right. Your church is nothing but a humanistic organization, only focused on people's physical needs. My mother's church understands that the spiritual life is far more important. After all, the physical world is temporary while the spiritual world lasts forever. The more you talk, the more you make me even more worried about the spiritual condition of your own soul. Can't you see my concern is for you? For where you'll spend eternity?"

Maria pulled her hand away from Robert's and folded her arms. "If you think there's any chance that I'm going to believe this 'salvation by faith' stuff, let me tell you right now — that will *never* happen. I have no doubt that the only thing that will matter on Judgment Day is how much love we have shown those around us — nothing more, nothing less. Salvation by faith is a sorely mistaken idea."

Robert felt himself even more empowered. "If you don't think that I love you enough to take a stand on your behalf, then you're the one sorely mistaken. I need you to be saved before we get married. And I need to know that we're going to teach our children how to be saved as well. Nothing could be more important to our family."

Maria fidgeted for a moment, removed the ring from her finger, and put it onto the dashboard in front of Robert. "There's no way I'll bring any child of mine to a church that teaches him to be afraid of God, to be afraid of Hell, to be afraid of the Beast of Revelation, and to be afraid of some horrible end of the world that supposedly could come at any moment. I won't allow my child to attend any church that teaches him to live in fear."

Robert pocketed the ring without responding. He got out of the car, walked to the passenger side, and opened the door for Maria.

"That's it?" Maria said. "Three years together, wedding plans, our entire future laid out for us, and you're throwing it all away just like that?"

It took every ounce of courage he could muster to turn and walk away from Maria, and not to turn back when he heard her beginning to sob before he started the car and drove off.

¤ ¤ ¤

After dropping her bags in her room, Maria left straightaway for the university's office building. Once inside, she made a beeline for Dr. Donald Richmond's office — the professor of religious history. Disregarding the sign that indicated he was not currently holding office hours for students, she burst into his office, closed the door, and broke into tears.

"What's wrong?" he said, moving to comfort her.

Through her heaving sobs, she was finally able to say, "Uncle Donny, Robert and I just broke up."

"I'm so sorry. What happened?"

"He's joined one of those 'born again' churches. And he said if I don't join it, then he won't marry me. He said he would feel responsible if our children and I are left behind to face the Beast of Revelation when Jesus returns."

"So why don't you just join his church and save the relationship?"

"You saw how that religion wore on Mom and Dad's relationship!" Maria exclaimed. "Remember how afraid of Hell she was because Dad didn't believe in marriage and wouldn't marry her; so she constantly nagged Dad and me to 'be saved.' And remember how every time there was an earthquake or a tsunami, she would run to check the Rapture Index online, always nervous about the 'end of the world.' I'm not going to have my children growing up like that. I want my children to know that God is a God of love — pure and simple. And I don't want Robert to be stressing me out all the time like Mom did to Dad."

"Well, you know how highly I think of Robert," Dr. Richmond said. "Otherwise, I wouldn't have introduced you to him."

"You think all the history majors are special," Maria joked through her tears.

"True! But Robert is extra special. He not only has an unusual passion for ancient history, but even more importantly, he's a man of principle — always trying to get to the truth. That's what I admire about him."

"Of course you do, because he reminds you so much of yourself."

Dr. Richmond hugged his niece even harder. "I'm so sorry to see you going through all this."

Another tear fell from Maria's face. "Because of Robert's principles, I know he'll never come back to me as long as he believes our marriage could harm me in any way. And as long as he believes in this salvation by faith and Rapture stuff, then our relationship is over.

I just don't know what to do."

Dr. Richmond paced the room and thought for a few moments, and then snapped his fingers. "You've got nothing to worry about. I know exactly what to do."

"I'd be indebted forever."

"Robert has a birthday coming up, right?"

"Yes, in about a week," Maria affirmed, with a quizzical look.

"Then you're going to give him the perfect gift, a gift that will solve everything."

Chapter 6

One week later, Robert was lying on his bed, staring up at the ceiling, completely absorbed by the memories of his last birthday. He saw his mother's face so clearly, the image of her smiling — even through her pain — as she lit the candles on his birthday cake a year ago to the day. It was almost too much to bear. He wondered if such a vivid memory of her would fade over time, whether the agony of missing her on a daily basis would lessen, and he would be able to sleep without waking to the nightmare that was her absence for the rest of his earthly days.

And there were the other nightmares as well — horrible, sweat-inducing dreams on a nightly basis of Maria being left behind after the Rapture, forced to submit to the Beast of Revelation. The very real possibility of her suffering eternal damnation when she could do something about it now — and live the rest of her life in a blissful marriage with him — left Robert feeling physically ill when he woke in the mornings.

A knock on his dorm room door startled him. "Come in!" he called out, sitting up.

Maria entered.

The sight of her sent a wave of contradictory emotions washing over him: love for her, missing her, yet still feeling sorry for her — and himself — for the permanent separation he was almost certain they would have to endure. But he managed a good-natured grin.

Maria walked over and handed the wrapped packets to Robert. "Happy birthday!" she said. They were the first words he had heard from her since the night in the parking lot. They sounded so sweet.

"Thanks for remembering," Robert said, his smile growing even wider. "You mind if I open the present now?"

Maria nodded enthusiastically.

Robert unwrapped his present: a Koine Greek Bible (the original Christian Bible) and a Koine Greek Bible Concordance (a book that lists where every Koine Greek word is used in the Bible).

He enthusiastically began studying the Greek Bible and concordance, flipping through pages, turning the books over in his hands. After a moment, he looked up at Maria, beaming. "Please tell me this is your way of showing me that you want to become a real Bible-believing Christian."

Maria sighed. "No, Robert. And I didn't come here to have an argument. I just know how much you love ancient history and ancient languages. And given your new interest in Christianity, I thought you'd want to study the Bible in its original language... that's all."

Robert decided not to push the point when she was trying to be nice. "Well, I really couldn't imagine a more perfect gift," he replied. "From now on, every time I learn a Greek word in class, I'll use the concordance to find the places where that word is used in the Bible. That way, I can learn the Greek language and the Bible at the same time. Thank you so much."

Maria was choking back tears.

Robert could tell that she was waiting for something. More words, perhaps. Or a hug. Some kind of an acknowledgement that there was still hope for their relationship. But something inside Robert prevented him from giving her what he knew she wanted.

After a few more moments of awkward silence, Maria said, "Well, I have things to do. I better go now."

¤ ¤ ¤

The next Sunday, Robert felt dreadfully self-conscious walking alone into the huge sanctuary of the evangelical church near campus, which was popular with the university students. Even though the ushers greeted him warmly, he felt out of place. He took a seat on the end of the aisle near the back and read the bulletin until the pastor began the service. For a few minutes, he wondered if he had made a mistake in coming, if his resolve was strong enough to do this alone — when his heart ached to have Maria by his side — and whether he could live a completely new life amongst people he did not even know. As the preparatory music stopped, indicating the service was about to begin, he felt the blush of shame, thinking of how his mother had died before seeing him saved and sitting in a true Christian church.

Right before the sermon, the pastor announced, "Every Sunday at this time, we take a moment to greet one another. Please say 'Hello' and shake the hand of everyone around you."

As soon as the organist started playing 'Because He Lives', the congregants rose to their feet to greet one another. After shaking hands with the people on his left and right, Robert turned around to find himself standing face-to-face with an exceptionally beautiful, radiant young woman. The young woman reached out her hand. "Hi! I'm Valerie."

Robert was awestruck for a moment. Quickly regaining his composure, he replied, "Hi. I'm Robert."

"Welcome, Robert. I don't recall ever seeing you here before."

"It's my first Sunday... In fact, I'm a new Christian, and just started attending church..." Robert stopped himself, feeling he was starting to ramble a bit too much.

"So, you're here alone?" Valerie asked.

"Yes. I don't have any Christian friends in town."

"Well, you've got one now." Valerie reached into her pocket and whipped out her cell phone. "Give me your number and I'll text you with mine. My dad's the pastor here. I'm staying in town at my parent's place, to save money until I leave for a missionary trip later this year. You can call me anytime with any questions you might have."

"Okay," Robert said, with a nervous smile, and then he gave her his number.

The conversation ended abruptly as the song finished, and the pastor approached the microphone ready to start the sermon.

The pastor began. "Now that we are in the end times, I find myself preaching more and more from the last book of the Bible — the book of Revelation — the book that details God's plan for the apocalyptic end of the world. And perhaps the question that I get asked the most is, 'Pastor, who is the Beast of Revelation? Who is the man represented by the devil's number, 666?' So today, I'm going to start my sermon by sharing with you what the Bible has to say about the identity of this demonic individual."

Robert was sitting on the edge of his seat.

If anyone has insight, let him calculate the number of the Beast, for it is a man's number. His number is 666.[5]

Then the preacher explained. "The Bible says that only those who are given special insight from God can know who the Beast is. John, the author of Revelation, was telling his readers that the identity of the horrible Beast was going to remain a mystery to most of humanity until the day the Beast emerges on the scene. So, 'who is the Beast?' I don't know. And according to the Bible, I can't know. And if that's the way God wants it, then that's the way it will be."

After all that buildup, Robert felt a little deflated. Ever since becoming a Christian, he had been wondering who the Antichrist — the Beast of Revelation — was going to be. Now he realized that he was never going to know. The Bible clearly said that it was a mystery that only those with special insight would be able to know.

¤ ¤ ¤

Over the next three weeks, Robert didn't have any contact with Maria. As badly as he wanted to be with her, he was determined to give her the space she needed to realize how wrong she had been about her church and the Bible. And he needed the time to help build his resolve to remain apart from her forever, if she refused to become saved.

Then on a Tuesday afternoon, Robert attended his Ancient Greek Language class. As a senior, much of the class was dedicated to advanced language topics, such as idioms and cultural expressions.

The teacher began. "Today, we're going to talk about the ancient Greek idiom: 'to have a mind.' The early Greeks used this expression in the same way we use the phrase 'anybody with half a brain.' In fact, the early Greeks used the opposite phrase, 'to not have a mind' when speaking about the senseless and the insane."

Robert took copious notes throughout the class, as usual. And when class ended, he rushed to his dorm room to start his daily Bible study.

Robert was delighted that the concordance showed that the Greek phrase 'to have mind' was in the Bible. And he was even more thrilled when he realized the phrase was used in the passage in Revelation that describes the identity of the dreaded Beast of Revelation. He grabbed his Greek Bible, and opened it to the passage. But when he read the sentence in Greek, applying what he had learned in class, he felt odd. Then he started feeling numb and then started shaking. He reread the sentence over and over again:

> Let **anyone who has a mind** calculate the number of the Beast. For it is a man's number. And his number is 666.[6]

In an effort to wrap his brain around what the Greek Bible said, Robert took a piece of paper and wrote out a direct translation of the sentence:

> Let **anybody with half a brain** calculate the number of the Beast. For it is a man's number. And his number is 666.[7]

"This doesn't make any sense," Robert said to himself. "According to the original Greek Bible, anybody with half a brain will know who the Beast of Revelation is, and only the senseless and the insane won't be able to figure it out. Not only does the original Bible say it's not a mystery — it says the answer is as obvious as the nose on the reader's face."

Robert sat for a while, thinking about the implications of what he had just read. It was then when he had his 'Eureka' moment. "If the author of Revelation expected every first century reader with half a brain to know the identity of the Beast, then he couldn't have been writing about anyone in the distant future. He must have been writing about someone they were all already familiar with — someone in the first century."

The implied logic slapped him in the face. "But the Beast of Revelation is inextricably tied to the teaching of the Rapture," he uttered. "And if the Beast of Revelation has already come and gone, that would mean there can't be any Rapture. And if that's the case, then everything I saw in that movie at Mom's church is fiction."

Robert stared at the translation. "Oh God! Have I made a big mistake with Maria?" he wondered.

---

6 Revelation 13:18 Greek literal
7 Revelation 13:18 Greek with idiom translated

Chapter 7

As Robert pondered the questions raised by the translation, he saw his phone on the desk and remembered Valerie's offer to answer any questions he might have. A quick phone call and he had a meeting that evening arranged at Sammy's, at Valerie's suggestion. Robert knew the area well, as it was only a few blocks from Maria's sorority house.

The hostess led Robert and Valerie over to a window seat. After they had both ordered, Robert explained the Greek idiom 'anyone who has a mind.' Then he showed Valerie that Revelation says that 'anybody with half a brain' will know who the Beast of Revelation is by the number 666.

Valerie was completely unfazed. "I can see why you would think the statement is mistranslated based on what you learned in class," she said with a laugh. "But when you think about it, the sentence itself shows that it truly is a mystery, not something the first century readers were expected to know."

"How can you be so sure?"

"Because, just as you said, the author of Revelation used a very cryptic, complex cipher based on the number 666. Obviously, he would never have used such an unsolvable riddle if he expected 'anybody with half a brain' to know who he was writing about."

Robert nodded. "I don't know why I didn't think of that before. It was right in front of me the whole time. I'm so glad I have you to talk to."

Valerie blushed.

As Robert reached for his glass of soda, he glanced to his right and almost jumped out of his seat. He saw Maria staring teary-eyed through the window at him and Valerie.

¤ ¤ ¤

The sight of Robert having dinner with a beautiful girl was

simply unbearable for Maria. The thought of Robert going out with someone else was absolutely the last thing she would have expected. Her first instinct was to run and cry. But she stopped herself, then she took a deep breath and stormed into the restaurant, telling herself that there was no way she was going to lose him to this woman.

"So nice to bump into you," she said to Robert, through her forced smile.

"It's great to see you, too!" He motioned toward Valerie. "Maria, I'd like you to meet Valerie. She's the pastor's daughter of the new church I'm going to. She's very smart and knows the Bible inside and out. Maybe she can show you what the Bible says about being a real Christian."

Maria was about to snap. But when she saw the adoring expression on Valerie's face, Maria forced herself to stifle the urge to respond, and instead, calmed herself and let Robert continue saying whatever he wanted.

Robert told Valerie, "Maria's church teaches that being a Christian is simply a matter of loving other people. Her pastor says that on Judgment Day, the only deciding factor will be how well we took care of other people's needs while we were alive."

"Ah!" Valeria exclaimed. "You go to one of those liberal churches! I'm not sure if you would even be interested in what the Bible has to say. After all, the teachings of the Bible aren't that important to liberals."

Maria took a step forward. "Oh, quite the contrary. Although my church is proudly 'liberal,' we actually use the Bible every Sunday."

"I'm sure your church uses a couple parts of it," Valerie said, in an unambiguously condescending manner. "But the biggest problem with liberal churches is that they throw out all the passages that they don't agree with — which is almost the entire Bible."

Maria looked at Robert. He was so engaged in the conversation. She knew if she was ever going to reach him, this was a critical moment. "Move over," she told Robert, and then she sat next to him. "So," she replied with feigned interest. "What parts of the Bible do we throw out?"

Valerie grinned. "Take salvation by faith, for example, which the Bible repeats over and over again. It's repeated so many times, it's impossible to miss. Yet Robert just said your church teaches the opposite, that salvation is determined by what you do. But according to Jesus, there's only one way to salvation — the narrow road."

Maria screwed up her face. "The what?"

Valerie looked at Robert. "You mean to tell me that you don't know one of the most popular parables in the entire Bible, the story Jesus taught about the narrow road and the broad road?"

"Not really," Maria admitted.

Valerie explained. "Jesus taught that there are two roads: the narrow road and the broad road. The narrow road is faith in Christ and it leads to life. And every other path, including trying to earn your way into heaven, is part of the broad road which leads to destruction. Jesus used the parable of the narrow road to teach people that there's one — and only one — way that leads to life. People aren't free to pick and choose how they get to heaven."

"I have to admit that I'm not all that familiar with that parable," Maria said. "In fact, I have to admit I'm not that familiar with the Bible at all."

Robert's shoulders began to sag.

"But I do know someone who is very familiar with it — my pastor," Maria continued. "Do you mind if I check with him on what you just said and get back to you?"

"Actually, I think that would be a wonderful idea," Valerie swiftly answered back.

Maria looked to Robert for support, but he wasn't giving any. He was clearly enthralled with this new woman.

"Are you sure you want to start a theological debate?" he said to Maria.

"Frankly, I don't think it'll be much of a debate at all," Valerie cut in. "Liberal Christians don't use the Bible. And if Maria doesn't know this yet, I'll be glad to point out the obvious to her."

Without even waiting for a response, Maria stood up rapidly, knocking a tray of drinks out of the waitress's hand and into the lap of a customer.

Maria was mortified. She looked at the waitress and pleaded, "I'm so sorry."

Much to her surprise, Patricia, the waitress, gave her a warm look and said, "Don't worry, accidents happen."

Maria all but ran from the restaurant.

¤ ¤ ¤

The restaurant manager ran straight over to Patricia while she was cleaning up the spill and apologizing profusely to the wet customer.

"You know you're already on thin ice," the manager yelled.

Patricia bowed her head and bit her tongue. "Yes, sir."

"If your kid wasn't so sick, I'd fire you right now," the manager said, while shaking his finger in her face. "But this isn't a pity party; it's a place of business. I'm warning you, if your family situation causes you to get distracted again or interferes with your work in any way, you won't be here for much longer. Either get your act together, or get out!"

Bowing her head even further, Patricia walked away.

¤ ¤ ¤

Still hurting from the insults she had suffered in the restaurant, Maria knocked furiously on the open door of her pastor's office.

The pastor looked up and smiled. "I'm here! Come in."

Maria entered and sat on the chair opposite the pastor's desk. She had never been in his office before. Looking up at the wall behind him, she saw an oversized poster with the pastor's favorite words: *Only one commandment, only one deciding factor — love one another.* Maria laughed to herself. She had heard those words so many times during the Sunday sermons.

As Maria's mind drifted back to her conversation with Valerie and her unsuccessful attempt to reach Robert, she felt a hot tear running down her face.

"What is it, Maria? You know that whatever it is, I'll help you in any way I can."

Maria explained what happened to her relationship with Robert after he had become a born-again Christian. "I ache for him," she said, baring her soul. "I can't live without him, but he won't let me get close now that he has his new church... and new friends." She then explained her conversation with Valerie — how Valerie had used her apparent superior knowledge of the Bible against her.

The pastor raised an eyebrow. "You've attended this church long enough to know that the entire New Testament, the section of the Bible written by Jesus' first followers, always goes back to: *Only one commandment, only one deciding factor — love one another,"* the pastor said, pointing back at the poster. "That's why I end every sermon by having the congregation recite these words. I want all of you to always remember this is the message Jesus sacrificed his blood to deliver."

"But according to Valerie, the Bible says the narrow road that leads to life is 'salvation by faith.'"

"Oh really?" the pastor mused. He pushed a box of tissue papers across the desk for Maria.

The pastor rose from his chair and walked over to his filing cabinet. After thumbing through some files, he pulled out a piece of paper.

Then the pastor explained. "Let me share with you one of the most important archaeological findings of recent times — the first century Aramaic Targums. This mega-discovery has shed profound light on the meaning of many passages in the Bible — including Jesus' teaching of the narrow road that leads to life."

"What are Aramaic Targums?" asked Maria.

"The first century Jews were raised to revere two sets of books: their scriptures and their Targums (books which contained the official interpretation of each scripture). Thanks to the Targums, we know what the religious leaders were teaching the Jews during the time of Christ. And it's surprising how much light they shed on so many of Jesus' teachings — most notably, his teaching of the narrow road."

The pastor handed Maria a paper containing a popular first century Targum entry:

> **For the wicked he prepared Gehenna, which is like a sharp sword, destroying with both sides.** Within it, he prepared darts of fire and burning coals, enkindled for the wicked, to be avenged of them in the age to come because they did not follow the commandments of the Law in this age. **For the Law is the tree of life for all who study it — and anyone who follows its commandments lives** and endures as the tree of life in the age to come.[8]

The pastor explained. "From birth, first century Jews were repeatedly indoctrinated with the teaching that those who follow the Law are on the narrow path that leads to life and everyone else is on a broad path which ends in fiery destruction in Gehenna. It was to people who believed this that Jesus said:

---

8 *Aramaic Targum of Genesis,* entry for Genesis 3:24

In everything, therefore, treat people the same way you want them to treat you, for this is the Law and the Prophets. Enter through the narrow gate; for the gate is wide and the way is broad that leads to destruction, and there are many who enter through it. For the gate is small and the way is narrow that leads to life, and there are few who find it."[9]

The pastor continued. "Can you imagine the shock of the crowd when Jesus said this? Jesus had made an astonishing statement: treating others in the same way that we wanted to be treated is the Law, the one thing we must obey to be on the road to life.

"Now, many people, such as Valerie, may argue that Jesus must've believed there is more to religion than making the needs of others equal to our own. But if Jesus really believed there was more to salvation than loving our neighbors, he did his audience a big disservice. For the Targums show us that these folks understood his teaching in one way... and one way only. Every person present understood Jesus to be saying, 'Treating others the same way we want to be treated is the sole requirement for being on the road to life.' In a very profound way, Jesus taught them, in no uncertain terms, that in his Law, *there is only one commandment, only one deciding factor — love one another.*"

The pastor wrote the following on a piece of paper and handed it to Maria:

According to the book of Matthew:

Treating others the way you want them to treat you is the Law.

Those who do this are on the narrow road that leads to life.

Those who do not do this are on the broad road that leads to destruction.

Therefore, according to the book of Matthew, *there is only one commandment, only one deciding factor — love one another.*

---

9   Matthew 7:12-14

Chapter 8

Patricia, the waitress from Sammy's, drove herself home in a daze from the restaurant after midnight. Completely exhausted after an eight-hour shift on her feet, she could barely make it from the car to the house. But the first thing she did once she was through the front door was to check in on her son. "Thank God, he's sound asleep," she said to herself.

After grabbing a soda from the fridge, she slumped into a chair and emptied the tips from her pocket. She counted them: $54.35. "I can't take care of my son on this." She reached for the phone and dialed.

"Why the hell are you calling me so late?" the voice on the other end grumbled.

Patricia bit her tongue. "Jack, I've never asked you for anything for our son. But I really need your help coming up with money, so he can see a specialist. I'm very worried about him."

"I got my own life to worry about," Jack barked. "You've no right to call me so late, bothering me with your problems."

Patricia heard a click followed by the dial tone. She hung up, tucked her chin to her chest, and prayed. "Please, God. I'm not asking you for anything for myself, but please give me a miracle for my boy. Whatever I have to go through for that miracle to happen, I'm willing, so long as my son is taken care of. In Jesus' name, Amen."

¤ ¤ ¤

The next morning, Robert was still reeling from the events at the restaurant, as he opened his books and began to do his homework. The assignment for his Greek class involved translating various passages containing the Greek idioms 'to have a mind' and 'to not have a mind.'

As Robert thought about the meanings that his teacher had given him, he became increasingly agitated. "My professor has to be

wrong about the meanings of these idioms. After all, the Bible uses
these expressions opposite to the way she has taught us," he said to
himself.

After a couple more minutes, Robert closed his books. "I need
to talk to Professor Harrison about this. She should know that she's
not teaching us the correct meanings."

¤ ¤ ¤

That same morning, Maria called Valerie and gleefully
informed her that the Aramaic Targums reveal that the very heart
of Jesus' teaching of the narrow road was that treating others as you
would have them treat you — the Golden Rule[10] — is the narrow road
that leads to life, not 'salvation by faith.'

Valerie flipped opened her Bible and read the passage herself.
"I didn't realize the narrow road was stated as being the Golden
Rule," she mumbled. "Interesting, but of course, that doesn't change
anything."

"What?" Maria asked, incredulously.

"Maria, you can't just cherry pick one passage and throw out
the rest of the Bible. After all, your church's teaching on salvation
contradicts the most famous verse in the entire New Testament."

"Which verse?" Maria asked.

"John 3:16, of course, the most quoted verse in all of
Protestantism."

Maria had her Bible handy, ready for the conversation. She
opened it and read the passage.

> For God so loved the world that he gave his one and only son that **whoever
> believes in him shall not perish**…

Valerie gave Maria time to read the verse and then asked, "So,
Maria, tell me, according to John 3:16, who goes to heaven: those who
'follow the Golden Rule' or those who 'believe in Jesus'?"

Maria remained silent.

---

10 **golden rule** n. The biblical teaching that one should behave toward others as one would have others
behave toward oneself. - *The American Heritage® Dictionary of the English Language, Fourth Edition,*
Copyright © 2009 by Houghton Mifflin Company.

Valerie went for the jugular. "I agree with your pastor about one thing: there really is only one commandment, only one deciding factor. But unfortunately, your pastor teaches the wrong commandment, the wrong deciding factor. There's good reason why John 3:16 is the cornerstone of every Bible-believing Protestant church, because it so clearly teaches that those who have faith in Jesus are the ones who will not perish. If salvation was dependent on doing good things to other people, then it would not be based on faith, like John 3:16 says it is."

Valerie waited patiently for Maria's reply.

After a minute of silence, Maria finally spoke up. "I keep reading the verse over and over again... and it seems that you're right."

Chapter 9

"I think you might have taught us the wrong meaning of a Greek idiom," Robert nervously blurted out to his professor in her office.

Professor Harrison cracked a half smile in what seemed to Robert like bemusement. "Well, I'm always willing to learn new things, Robert. So please, tell me what my star student has discovered."

The professor's response put Robert at ease, although he wasn't sure that she was taking him seriously. "I found a first century document that uses an idiom in the exact opposite way that you said the expression was used."

"Let me tell you that I couldn't be more delighted that you're reading Greek texts above and beyond the homework I give you. So, which idiom are you talking about?"

"To have mind."

The professor leapt from her chair, walked over to the bookshelf, and grabbed two books. She flipped through the first book, a very big book. Then, pointing to an entry on a page, she said, "I assume you didn't look up the expression in a *Greek English Lexicon* by Liddell and Scott, which you know is the most authoritative dictionary of Greek. Notice the entry for the idiom 'to have mind'? Why don't you read the primary meaning aloud?"

Robert read, "To have *sense*, be *sensible*."[11]

The teacher nodded. "So, just as you learned in class, the idiom has to do with having common sense and sensibility. That's why I told you it's similar to the English slang, 'anybody with half a brain', as this slang means, 'anyone with common sense.'" The professor opened the second book entitled *In and Out of the Mind*. She pointed to a paragraph, and once again, asked Robert to read it aloud.

"People who act with nous [the Greek word for mind], and 'have' it, are sensible. People who do not are senseless, unwise, insane."[12]

---

11 νοῦν ἔχειν : a) to have *sense*, be *sensible*, *Greek English Lexicon*, by Liddell and Scott, p. 1180
12 *In and Out of the Mind*, by Ruth Padel, 1994, p. 32

The professor nodded once again. "So you see, Robert, 'to not have mind' meant 'to be senseless, unwise, insane,' just as I taught you. Both expressions mean exactly what you learned in class."

"But that just doesn't make any sense," Robert blurted out. "Why then would a first century writer say anybody with half a brain — anyone who isn't senseless or insane — would know who he was referring to when he gave 'the man's number'?"

The teacher laughed. "But of course a first century writer would say only a half-wit wouldn't know who he was referring to. For in first century Greek, everyone was identified by both their name and their number."

"I don't understand."

"In a week, we'll be discussing this topic in great detail in class. But I'd be glad to give you a brief overview of why only an insane individual in the first century would not know the identity of a person by that person's number."

"Okay."

The professor walked over to her filing cabinet and pulled out a sheet of paper with the following on it:

Symbol	Character	Number
A	A	1
B	B	2
Γ	G	3
Δ	D	4
E	E	5
F	V, W	6
Z	Z	7
H	Ē	8
Θ	Th	9
I	I	10
K	K	20
Λ	L	30
M	M	40
N	N	50
Ξ	X	60
O	O	70
Π	P	80
Ϙ	Q	90
P	R	100
Σ	S	200
T	T	300
Υ	Y, U	400
Φ	Ph	500
X	Ch	600
Ψ	Ps	700
Ω	Ō	800
Ϡ	(Sanpi)	900

The professor explained the chart. "In the first century, every Greek symbol represented both a letter and a number *at the same time*. For example, the first symbol in the chart represented both the letter 'A' and the number '1' *at the same time*. Because of this duality, the collection of symbols comprising a person's identity represented a collection of letters (the person's name) and a collection of numbers (the number of the person's name) *at the same time*.

"For example, let's consider Jesus of Nazareth, a very famous individual from the first century. Jesus was identified by the Greek symbols: **Ι Η Σ Ο Υ Σ**. And these symbols represented both Jesus' Greek name (IĒSOUS) and the number of Jesus' name (888) [10 + 8 + 200 + 70 + 400 + 200] *at the same time*. So, whenever a first century Greek saw those symbols, he thought of both Jesus' name and the number of his name each time. People's names and the number of their names were inextricably linked to one another."

"I can see from the chart that early Greek symbols were letters and numbers at the same time," Robert concurred. "But do we have any archaeological evidence that they actually used both the letters and the numbers to identify people?"

"Very good question as usual, Robert!" the professor exclaimed. She walked back to her filing cabinet and returned with yet another handout. "Here's an example from a late first century Christian writing."

> And then the child of the great God to man shall come incarnate, being fashioned like mortals on the earth… 888 will the name **reveal** to men who are giving up to unbelief.[13]

The professor looked up at Robert. "In this first century document, did the writer say he was *concealing* or *revealing* the person's identity with the number 888?"

Robert read the excerpt. "The number was used to *reveal* the person's identity."

"Precisely. In this Christian writing, the number of Jesus' name was used to *reveal* his identity, not to hide it. The writer of this document wanted unbelievers to know precisely whom he was talking about. That's why he wrote '888 will the name *reveal*'. And quite literally, given Jesus' fame in the first century, only a senseless or insane person in that culture would not know who this document was referring to. And that must be the same situation with the document you are referring to. If the writer said 'anyone who has a mind' will know who a person is by their number, then you can be sure that the writer is referring to the number of a very prominent, very famous, person of that time. That's the meaning of the passage you are translating."

"Wow!" Robert exclaimed. "Thank you."

---

13 *The Sibylline Oracles, Book I*, lines 393 - 399

"You're very welcome. And I'm sure you'll find next week's class on this matter even more interesting and more enlightening. There was so much going on during this time regarding people's names and numbers — fascinating things."

Robert shook the professor's hand and headed to the door.

¤ ¤ ¤

When Robert returned to his dorm room, he was excited on one hand, yet upset on the other. He was excited that he might be able to find out who the Beast of Revelation was. Yet he was upset at the thought that Valerie's Bible had mistranslated the sentence. And he was also upset that her church didn't teach her how numbers were used to reveal people's identities in the first century. Instead, her church taught that numbers were used as complex riddles — the exact opposite of the way they were used in the first century.

Robert shook off his concern. "So the Book of Revelation wanted to reveal the identity of the Beast… not conceal it. And the number 666 must refer to an extremely prominent person — which is why Revelation's author wrote that only an idiot won't know who he was referring to. This means, the identity of the Beast can be solved with certainty. I *can* know who the Beast is."

Robert pondered all he had learned. Then he added the following entry to his journal:

CLUES TO THE BEAST OF REVELATION:

The number of the beast's name is 666, which means the sum of the symbols of his name is 666.

Anybody with half a brain will know him by this number, which means the beast was so popular that only a crazy person wouldn't recognize him by the number 666.

Chapter 10

Robert called Valerie to inform her of how numbers were commonly used in the first century to reveal — not conceal — people's identities. Then he explained why he's more convinced than ever that her Bible is translated incorrectly.

"I'm at my dad's house right now," Valerie stammered in response. "Why don't you come over and we can all talk about it here?"

"Sure… I don't have classes until this afternoon," Robert replied. "See you soon."

¤ ¤ ¤

Patricia's 13-year-old son, Jack Jr., emerged from his bedroom and sat down at the breakfast table.

"Good morning, honey," Patricia said brightly, before giving him a kiss on the forehead. "I'll have your eggs ready in a jiffy."

During breakfast, Patricia and Jack were joking and laughing, when all of a sudden, Jack fell to the floor — eyes closed, his body completely motionless.

Patricia almost choked on the orange juice that was still in her mouth. She spit it out and ran over to her son.

"Jack! Jack!" Patricia yelled, while vigorously shaking his body.

Jack slowly opened his eyes. "Mom… What happened?"

"I don't know, honey, but we're going to the emergency room right now."

¤ ¤ ¤

Robert didn't know if he was so nervous because he was in the home of this fascinating new woman, Valerie, or because he had been summoned to a meeting after calling to inform her that her Bible was translated incorrectly.

Valerie's father started right in. "I hope you don't mind, but Valerie shared with me all your questions regarding the Beast of Revelation. And I understand, given what little you know about the Beast, why you think he could be somebody from the past. But I'm sure once you learn a little more about him, then you'll understand that he has to be somebody in the future. Would you like to see a passage in the Bible that specifically says that the Beast is going to be someone in the future?"

Chapter 11

Maria sat across the desk of her pastor and said, haltingly, "Robert's friend, Valerie, showed me John 3:16, which says that everyone who has faith in Jesus will go to heaven. Valerie says this verse proves there is only one commandment — to have faith in Jesus. And she says your teaching of 'the one commandment' contradicts what Jesus taught in the book of John."

The pastor smiled. "Let me show you something Saint Cyril of Alexandria, one of the earliest Christian scholars, wrote."

The pastor pulled the following from his filing cabinet and showed it to Maria:

> Since the **love of neighbor contains and accomplishes the fulfillment of all the commands of our Savior**, how should not the man who fulfills this commandment sincerely and blamelessly be regarded as truly marvelous[14]

The pastor then said, "Do you have any idea which writing of Saint Cyril's this is taken from?"

"No."

"It's from his commentary on the book of John, the Biblical book containing John 3:16. According to this prominent early Christian scholar, the book of John teaches that the 'love of neighbor contains and accomplishes the fulfillment of all the commands of our Savior."

"Where in the book of John does it say this?" Maria asked, moving to the edge of her seat.

The pastor opened his Bible. "Saint Cyril wrote this when he was commenting on this passage."

> **If you keep my commandments, you shall abide in my love**; even as I have kept my Father's commandments, and abide in his love. These things have I spoken unto you, that my joy might remain in you, and that your joy might

---

14 Saint Cyril of Alexandria, *On The Gospel According to Saint John, Book X*, Section on John 15:12

be full. **This is my commandment, that you love one another, as I have loved you.**[15]

The pastor explained. "The book of John uses a shift from the plural — 'my commandments' — to the singular — 'my commandment.' The book of John does this to show that all of Jesus' commandments boil down to just one commandment: love one another. And this is why Saint Cyril wrote this when he was commenting on this passage."

"Interesting," Maria remarked.

"And even more interesting still is that the book of John quickly repeats this same sentiment to really drive the point home," said the pastor. "Unfortunately, however, the book of John's double down gets lost in translation."

The pastor read the following passage:

This is my command: Love each other. — John 15:17 NIV

Then the pastor explained. "The NIV Bible makes it sound like loving one another is just one command of Jesus', as if it is one of many commands Jesus gave. But Saint Cyril was reading the book of John in its native Greek, which reads:

These things I command, that you love one another.   John 15:17 Literal Greek

"In the original Greek text, Jesus taught, 'I command you all these things: that you love one another.' Jesus doubled down to drive home the point that all of his commandments really do boil down to one thing: love one another."

Maria looked up at the poster behind the pastor: *Only one commandment, only one deciding factor — love one another.* "So if this is the *only* commandment, then it must be the *only* deciding factor on the day of judgment... right?"

The pastor nodded. "But of course. In fact, the book of John makes this very clear in the very same passage that Saint Cyril wrote about." The pastor showed Maria the following:

---

15 John 15:10-12

If anyone does not abide in Me, he is thrown away as a branch and dries up; and they gather them, and cast them into the fire and they are burned… **If you keep my commandments, you shall abide in my love**; even as I have kept my Father's commandments, and abide in his love. These things have I spoken unto you, that my joy might remain in you, and that your joy might be full. **This is my commandment, that you love one another, as I have loved you.**[16]

The pastor continued. "According to the book of John, Jesus taught that only those who abide in him, by following his command to love one another, will avoid being thrown into the fire. This is the deciding factor. So you see, Maria, there really is *only one commandment, only one deciding factor — love one another.*"

The pastor noticed Maria had brought the sheet of paper from her previous visit. He asked her for it and added the teachings from the book of John:

According to the book of Matthew:

> Treating others the way you want them to treat you is the Law.

> Those who do this are on the narrow road that leads to life.

> Those who do not do this are on the broad road that leads to destruction.

Therefore, according to the book of Matthew, *there is only one commandment, only one deciding factor — love one another.*

According to the book of John:

> Those who abide in Jesus (by following his commandments) will have life.

> Those who do not abide in Jesus (by not following his commandments) will be thrown into the fire.

> Jesus has only one commandment: love one another.

---

16 John 15:6, 10-12

Therefore, according to the book of John, *there is only one commandment, only one deciding factor — love one another.*

Chapter 12

"The doctor will see your son now," the nurse in the emergency room told Patricia after an agonizing three-hour wait.

"Finally," Patricia sighed.

Patricia explained how her son had collapsed at the breakfast table.

The doctor looked her son over, gave him a quick physical, and then said, "He seems fine now."

"That's it?" Patricia shouted. "Can't you run some tests to figure out what's happening to him? This is serious!"

The doctor furrowed his eyebrows and said quietly. "Listen, you don't have any insurance. And your son doesn't appear to be in any immediate danger. There's nothing more I can do."

The doctor sped off without even waiting for a response.

Patricia hugged Jack. "It's going to be okay. I promise."

Patricia accompanied her son home in a cab, then rushed to the restaurant, applying makeup in the back of the taxi.

"You're late!" Patricia's boss yelled, as she entered Sammy's.

"Yes, but…"

"I don't want to hear it! If you're going to be late again, don't bother showing up, because if you come here late one more time — by even one minute — you don't have a job here anymore!"

¤ ¤ ¤

Maria sighed. "I now understand that the fifteenth chapter of John says that loving others is Jesus' one and only commandment. But that only confuses me even more. After all, the third chapter of John says, 'whoever *believes* in Jesus will not perish'. Doesn't that mean all a person has to do is to *believe*? Isn't that salvation by *faith*?"

The pastor took out a piece of paper and wrote the following:

'Believe in the doctor and your life will be saved' means 'Do what the doctor

41

says and your life will be saved.'

'Believe in the marriage counselor and your relationship will be saved' means 'Do what the marriage counselor says and your relationship will be saved.'

'Believe in the financial advisor and your nest egg will be saved' means 'Do what the financial advisor says and your nest egg will be saved.'

Then the pastor explained. "Doctors, marriage counselors, and financial advisors are all authority figures. Even in English, the phrase 'believe in' means 'obey' when it is applied to an authority figure. When the topic is an authority figure, it means 'do what they say'. And the Greek phrase used in John 3:16 was even stronger. When applied to an authority figure, the phrase expresses, 'trust the authority figure enough to do what he says.' Let me give you an example right from the third chapter of John."

The pastor opened an NASB Bible to John chapter three, verse thirty-six, and showed it to Maria.

He who **believes in** the Son has eternal life; but he who **does not obey** the Son will not see life, but the wrath of God abides on him.[17]

Then he explained. "The underlined phrase in this passage is the Koine word *apeitheia* in the original Bible. And in the tons of Koine Greek documents discovered, this word had *a fixed meaning from which it never deviated.*[18] The word expressed 'disobedience, rebellion, contumacy.' This means the third chapter of John is contrasting 'those who trust Jesus enough to do what he says' versus 'those who refuse to do what he says'. A more true-to-the-Greek translation of John 3:16 is:

For God so loved the world that he gave his only Son that **whoever trusts him enough to do what he says will not perish…**

"Unfortunately, the full meaning of the Koine Greek word is hidden from modern readers."

Maria lit up. "Then 'to believe in the Son' means to do what he

17 John 3:36 NASB
18 "That this noun… connotes **invariably** 'disobedience, rebellion, contumacy,' is made abundantly clear from papyri and inscriptions." *Vocabulary of the Greek Testament*, Moulton and Milligan, p. 55

says —'to love one another' just like he told us to."

The pastor nodded. Then he showed Maria the following passage written by John himself:

> And this is God's command: to **believe in the name of his Son Jesus Christ and [therefore] love one another just as he commanded us.**[19]

The pastor explained. "John understood the meaning of John 3:16 very well. He understood that believing in the Son meant doing what he said — loving one another just as he commanded us."

Maria looked up at the poster again: *Only one commandment, only one deciding factor: love one another.* "So John believed that those who do what Jesus said — those who love one another — are the ones who will not perish? John believed loving others will be the deciding factor on Judgment Day?"

"Absolutely," the pastor replied. Then he showed Maria another passage written by John:

> We know we have passed out of death into life **because we love the brethren.** He who does not love abides in death.[20]

Then the pastor explained. "To John, loving others was the very basis of salvation. It was the deciding factor of whether a person perishes ('abides in death') or whether he has 'passed out of death into life.' This is how John himself understood the message of John 3:16. And we teach John's understanding of this verse in our church."

Maria sat back. "Got it!"

The pastor motioned for Maria to hand him the piece of paper one more time. He updated the paper with the teachings from the letter written by John:

According to the book of Matthew:

Treating others the way you want them to treat you is the Law.

Those who do this are on the narrow road that leads to life.

Those who do not do this are on the broad road that leads to

---

19 1 John 3:23
20 1 John 3:14

destruction.

Therefore, according to the book of Matthew, *there is only one commandment, only one deciding factor — love one another.*

According to the book of John:

> Those who abide in Jesus (by following his commandments) will have life.
>
> Those who do not abide in Jesus (by not following his commandments) will be thrown into the fire.
>
> Jesus has only one commandment: love one another.

Therefore, according to the book of John, *there is only one commandment, only one deciding factor — love one another.*

According to the book of 1ˢᵗ John:

> This is God's commandment: to trust the Son enough to love one another, just as he commanded.
>
> By loving others, we know we have passed from death to life.
>
> For it is those who do not love others who remain in death.

Therefore, according to the book of 1ˢᵗ John, *there is only one commandment, only one deciding factor — love one another.*

Chapter 13

Meanwhile, Robert was continuing his increasingly contentious conversation with Valerie and her father on the subject of the Beast of Revelation.

"Please cut to the chase, Pastor. Why are you so sure that the Beast is someone in the future?"

"Because," the pastor replied, "that's *the only* possible meaning of one of the riddles about the Beast."

"Which riddle?"Robert asked.

The pastor handed Robert a copy of the bestselling modern translation of the Bible — the New International Version — and asked Robert to read.

> **They are also seven kings. Five have fallen, one is,** the other has not yet come; but when he does come, he must remain for a little while. **The Beast** who once was, and now is not, **is an eighth king.** He belongs to the seven and is going to his destruction.[21]

Then the pastor explained. "Robert, notice that the Book of Revelation says that it is written during the reign of the sixth king; it says, 'five [kings] have fallen, one is'. Also notice that the Beast is going to be the 'eighth king'. In other words, during the reign of the sixth king, the passage is prophesying about a coming eighth king. Therefore, no matter how you interpret the riddle, you have to agree this prophecy was describing someone in the future. So it could not be referring to a person that the original readers were already familiar with — as your translation of Revelation would require. Make sense?"

Robert read the phrase 'eighth king' over and over before finally conceding. "It seems pretty cut and dry. But I still don't know why John wrote that only an imbecile wouldn't know who the Beast is and why John used the number of the Beast's name — a very common

---

21 Revelation 17:10-11 NIV

first century convention for revealing the identity of someone."

"You can't cherry pick around the riddle I just showed you," the pastor said, with a hint of condescension. "You have to take the Bible as a whole. That's the only way to get to the truth."

"Well, I do see that Revelation says the Beast will be 'an eighth king,'" said Robert. "So I must be missing something. And you certainly know more about the Bible than I do."

¤ ¤ ¤

Maria walked from the pastor's office back to her sorority, pondering all that he had shared. As she came within a couple blocks of the facility, she passed by Sammy's and noticed Valerie sitting alone at a booth. *Great!* she thought. *Now I can tell Valerie how John himself described John 3:16's command to believe in the Son, while I still have everything fresh in my mind.*

Maria entered the restaurant. On her way to the booth, she noticed the harried look on Patricia's face. Maria walked over to her. "Is everything okay?" she asked.

Maria assumed that the woman would politely tell her that everything was fine, but was shocked when Patricia let forth a sudden, forceful stream of words: "No! Everything is not okay! My son has a very serious medical condition and I can't get any doctor to help him without insurance!"

Maria saw that Patricia immediately regretted dumping her problems on a stranger. Maria put her arms around Patricia. "I don't know you. But I do care."

"Thank you," Patricia said, hugging back.

Maria reached into her pocket and withdrew her cell phone. "I'm not making any promises. But sometimes, the doctors who attend my church provide services free of charge for people in need. Can I get your number?"

After getting the information, Maria walked over to the booth where Valerie was seated and explained everything she had learned from her pastor.

To Maria's surprise, Valerie simply retorted, "I must admit, I've never thought of John 3:16 in that way. On the surface, it even seems to make sense. But I'm sure there must be something wrong with that interpretation."

"But aren't you disagreeing with John more than you're disagreeing with my church?" Maria asked. "After all, he's the one who taught that 'believing in the Son' means 'loving one another as the Son commanded'. And aren't you also disagreeing with Jesus who taught, in very clear first century lingo, that treating others the same way we want to be treated is the narrow road that leads to life?"

"I really don't have time right now for a debate," Valerie remarked. "I gotta go."

Valerie quickly scooted out of the booth, paid her check, and left.

¤ ¤ ¤

Robert was sitting in a lecture hall.

The professor began. "Today, we'll be discussing one of my favorite first century topics," the history lecturer said, "...the numbers of names." Professor Harrison passed out the same handout she had shared with Robert in her office and then explained how every first century Greek symbol represented both a letter and a number at the same time. She further explained how, therefore, every first century person was identified by both their name and the number of their name.

Robert was glad this day had finally arrived.

Professor Harrison continued. "As each of you go on to your individual careers as museum curators, archaeologists, or historians, it is critical that you are intimately familiar with 'the numbers of names', as you will find these numbers inscribed on archaeological finds from this period, as well as in the popular literature from this time. Take, for example, the archaeological excavation of the Roman city of Pompeii — the city instantly sealed in a sea of ash during the eruption of Mt. Vesuvius in 79 AD. And I want you to now consider an inscription discovered on one of the walls."

She gave her students a handout, which read:

I love her whose number is 545.[22]

---

22 *Studies in Biblical and Semitic Symbolism,* by Maurice H. Farbridge, p. 95

Professor Harrison then explained. "From this inscription, you can see the extreme commonness of identifying people by 'the number of their name'. And you can now see why you need to be familiar with the numbers of people's names when you are examining archaeological findings of this time."

She distributed another handout. "This paper contains another graffiti writing, this one from the marketplace walls of Pompeii."

Harmonia, the number of her honorable name is 45.[23]

The professor explained. "Here's a second archaeological finding referring to 'the number of a person's name'. In this finding, the writer of the riddle expected each passerby to figure out how the number 45 made Harmonia's name 'honorable'. So class, please tell me, what was it about the number 45 that made Harmonia's name honorable? And why did the writer expect the common, ordinary man and woman to know the answer to this riddle?"

The class remained silent. No one knew the answer.

Professor Harrison smiled. "The answer to this riddle, and others you will find from the first century, can only be solved with an understanding of *triangle numbers*." She passed out the following to her class:

---

23 *Studies in Biblical and Semitic Symbolism,* by Maurice H. Farbridge, p. 95

Unit	Triangle	Double Triangle
First	1	1
Second	3	6
Third	6	21
Fourth	10	55
Fifth	15	120
Sixth	21	231
Seventh	28	406
Eighth	36	666
Ninth	45	1035

Then she explained. "This table lists the first nine triangle and double triangle numbers — the most popular triangle numbers of the time. While I do not expect you to know how to calculate triangle numbers,[24] you will be quizzed on knowing the numbers in this table, as they were integral to the daily life of those living in the first few centuries."

A petite female student seated in the back raised her hand and asked, "I don't understand why these 'triangle numbers' would be necessary for anything."

The lecturer laughed. "I was just getting to that. Clement of Alexandria, a second century Father, wrote something very interesting about triangle numbers."

Professor Harrison passed around another sheet, which read:

The number 120 is a triangular number... **of one triangle, namely 15...** From the unity of the triangles, **the fifth becomes 15.**[25]

Then she explained. "I want you to focus your attention on

24 For a detailed discussion on how triangle and double triangle numbers were calculated and referenced in the first century see Appendix A.
25 Clement of Alexandria, *The Stromata*, Book VI, Chapter XI, excerpted from paragraphs 4 and 5

the fifth unit in the chart as you reread this passage from Clement of Alexandria."

Unit	Triangle	Double Triangle
First	1	1
Second	3	6
Third	6	21
Fourth	10	55
Fifth	15	120
Sixth	21	231
Seventh	28	406
Eighth	36	666
Ninth	45	1035

The lecturer continued. "Notice how double triangle number 120, triangle number 15, and the fifth unit are all on the same line — they are interrelated based on 'the unity of the triangles'. And it is this very interrelationship that Clement of Alexandria was writing about. And from this passage, we can see how Clement, a prominent Father, expected his readers to be familiar with triangles and double triangles *both*. For, in this passage, Clement reminded his readers that double triangle 120 is compounded 'of one triangle, namely 15' which is a 'fifth.'"

Professor Harrison passed out another sheet.

This number consists of **36**... which is a cube, and at the same time **a triangle**.[26]

The professor explained. "These words were written by Philo Judaeus, perhaps the most popular author of the first century. So can anyone tell me the significance of this?"

26 *Questions and Answers on Genesis, III*, by Philo Judaeus, paragraph 56

"Given that triangle numbers are mentioned by such a mass market writer, we can see how integral they were to first century daily life," a student called out.

The professor nodded. "Now, tell me, which unit of the triangles was Philo writing about in this passage?"

Robert looked down at the chart and found the number 36. He sat there, staring at the line on the chart where that number was found.

Unit	Triangle	Double Triangle
First	1	1
Second	3	6
Third	6	21
Fourth	10	55
Fifth	15	120
Sixth	21	231
Seventh	28	406
Eighth	36	666
Ninth	45	1035

Robert gulped and raised his hand. When the lecturer called on him, he said, "Philo is writing about the number 36. And 36 is 'an eighth.'"

Of course, Robert had noticed that 666 was 'an eighth' as well. Robert realized that 666 and 'an eighth' were interrelated in the first century based on the unity of triangles. And his mind started to race. "Is it possible that the Beast was called 'an eighth' based on the number of his name — 666?"

The lecturer continued her class. "You now have one more clue to solving the riddle that was scribbled on the marketplace wall in Pompeii. Let me remind you of the riddle: Harmonia, the number of her honorable name is 45."

Robert, along with all the students in the class, looked for the number 45 on the chart. He saw that 45 was 'a ninth'.

Unit	Triangle	Double Triangle
First	1	1
Second	3	6
Third	6	21
Fourth	10	55
Fifth	15	120
Sixth	21	231
Seventh	28	406
Eighth	36	666
Ninth	45	1035

The lecturer observed the knowing looks from her students.

Every student present raised their hands because the answer was now so obvious. The teacher called on the petite female student in the back, the one who originally wasn't sure why triangle numbers were so important.

"When the people in the marketplace saw Harmonia's number 45, they instantly knew it was 'a ninth,'" she said. "In ancient Rome, 'the ninth' was called *teleios* — it was called 'perfectly complete'[27] — and the perfectly complete 'ninth' served as an organizing principle for all of Roman life. The Roman calendar was organized around the *nones* — the 'ninth'[28]. Males were purified *the ninth* day after birth so *Nundina*, the goddess of the sacred ninth, could supposedly preside over the ceremony. But most importantly of all, at least in regards to the meaning of this riddle, the *nundinae* — every 'ninth day' — were

27 *The Pythagorean Triangle*, by George Oliver, p.209
28 *The ruins and excavations of ancient Rome*, by Rodolfo Amedeo Lanciani, p. 589

the marketplace days in ancient Rome.[29] The country folk would come into the city every *nundinae* (every ninth day) to sell their wares and to buy from others.[30] The graffiti artist expected those in the marketplace to recognize that the number of Harmonia's name is 'a ninth' based on the unity of the triangles, and that is what made her name so very honorable."

"Very good," Professor Harrison affirmed, with a grin. "And the archaeologists who uncovered this riddle solved it quickly because they were familiar with the triangle and double triangle numbers on the chart. And so you must be, too, in preparation for your future career."

The student smiled back in acknowledgement.

Robert didn't hear anything else that the lecturer said for the rest of the class. His mind was caught in a perpetual loop. The average, everyday first century person — anybody with half a brain — was expected to know that 45, the number of a person's name, is 'a ninth'. This means that anybody with half a brain would've also instantly recognized that 666, the number of a person's name, is 'an eighth'. So is it possible that triangle numbers can explain the passage describing the Beast? Robert couldn't wait to get back to his dorm room and grab his Greek version of the Bible.

¤ ¤ ¤

Robert didn't walk back to his dorm room — he ran back. Without even closing the door, he opened his Greek Bible to Revelation and started shaking in anger when he read what was actually written in the Greek:

And the Beast which was and is not — **out of the seven kings, he is an eighth** — and into destruction he is going.[31]

---

29 "As, however, the principal business of the day was buying and selling, the *nundinae* were exactly equivalent to our market day" *Urconium: A Historical Account of the Ancient Roman City, and of the Excavations Made Upon Its Site at Wroxeter*, by Thomas Wright, p.154.

30 "In time of peace he accustomed [free men] to remain at their tasks in the country, except when it was necessary for them to come to market, upon which occasions they were to meet in the city in order to traffic, and to that end **he appointed every ninth day for the markets**." Dionysius of Halicarnassus (Second Century BC), *Roman Antiquities*, 2.28.3

31 Revelation 17:11 Greek

Robert's mind was racing. "The Greek doesn't say the Beast is an eighth king. The Greek says that out of the seven kings, the Beast is an eighth — meaning *he is one of the seven kings, the one who is 'an eighth'*, in the same way that Harmonia was 'a ninth'."

Robert opened the bestselling modern Bible — the New International Version — and read how the passage was translated:

> **The Beast** who once was, and now is not, **is an eighth king**. He belongs to the seven and is going to his destruction.[32]

Robert became furious as he stared at the passage. "This Bible has shifted the words around to make it appear that the Greek calls the Beast 'an eighth king'. This Bible puts the word 'king' after the word 'eighth' — totally changing the meaning of the passage. That is simply unforgivable!"

After a few minutes, Robert's anger transformed to excitement, as he began to consider the possibilities. "Wait a minute! Thanks to what I learned in class, I can now figure out the meaning of the passages from Revelation."

CLUES TO THE BEAST OF REVELATION:

The number of the beast's name is 666, which means the sum of the symbols of his name is 666.

Anybody with half a brain will know him by this number, which means the beast was so popular that only a crazy person wouldn't recognize him by the number 666.

Out of the seven kings, he is an eighth, which means there is a list of seven kings, and the one whose name is 666 (an eighth), is the Beast.

---

32   Revelation 17:11 NIV

Chapter 14

Valerie was visiting her father in his office, trying to hide her nervousness. After some small talk about upcoming church events, she said, "Dad, I have a question about the Bible that I'd like your opinion on."

"Of course, honey."

Valerie opened her Bible and read:

> In everything, therefore, treat people the same way you want them to treat you, for this is the Law and the Prophets. Enter through the narrow gate... For the gate is small and the way is narrow that leads to life, and there are few who find it.[33]

Then Valerie said, "Jesus taught that *treating others the same way you want to be treated is the Law, the one thing that people must do to be on the narrow road to life.* Doesn't this mean it's the only thing he wants us to do in order to be saved?"

Her father shook his head. "Honey, even if Jesus considered loving our neighbors to be the total fulfillment of the Law, it wouldn't matter anyway."

"Why?"

"Because after Jesus left the earth, the Law was abolished. Therefore, none of Jesus' teachings regarding the Law matter."

"How can we be so sure of this?" Valerie asked.

"We know this from the letters Jesus' disciples wrote to their first converts — letters that are part of the Bible itself. In these letters, Jesus' disciples told their followers that they were not under any law whatsoever. They taught their converts that salvation comes from faith alone — the very opposite of being obligated to follow any law."

It all made so much sense to Valerie when her father explained it. "I knew there had to be a straightforward answer to all this."

---

33 Matthew 7:12-14 NASB

¤ ¤ ¤

Valerie listened to Robert over the phone as he enthusiastically shared all that he had learned about triangle numbers and the fact that the Greek Bible says the Beast is 'an eighth' — *not* 'an eighth king', as the popular New International Version of the Bible says.

Valerie was mortified. She put the phone on mute and looked up at her father. "Dad, I need your help!"

"What is it, honey?"

"Robert's now more convinced than ever that the Beast of Revelation is someone from the past. Is there anything else you can show him to prove that the Beast of Revelation is someone coming in the future?"

"Absolutely!"

Valerie took the phone off mute. "Do you mind coming by my father's office to explain to him what you just told me?" Valerie hung up the phone. "Dad, if Robert stops believing in the coming of the Beast of Revelation, then he'll stop believing in the Rapture, too. And if he doesn't believe in the Rapture, then he might start questioning everything, including Biblical salvation — and I might lose him."

Her father was startled. "Honey, I didn't know you were interested in Robert that way."

Valerie felt herself blush. "If Maria became a Christian, I would have to respect that. But if she's going to try to get him to join her liberal, humanistic, so-called 'church', that would be a waste. In that case, Robert is much better off with me. Can you imagine how much his knowledge of ancient languages and history will add to his understanding of the Bible? Wouldn't he make a great missionary!" Valerie began to daydream about the possibilities.

¤ ¤ ¤

The pastor was unmoved by Robert's analysis. "Robert, it doesn't matter how much these 'triangle numbers' may fit Revelation's riddle of the Beast, because there's still no possibility that the Beast could have been someone in the past."

"How can you be so sure?"

The pastor opened his Bible and showed Robert the following

passage:

> **All inhabitants of the earth will worship the Beast**—all whose names have not been written in the book of life.[34]

Then he asked, "Has there ever been a ruler who was worshipped by *all the inhabitants of the earth*?"

Robert thought a while before replying. "No. Never."

"And that's how I know for sure that the Beast must still be in the future, because this prophecy hasn't been fulfilled yet."

Robert folded his arms.

Valerie turned to Robert. "What could be more obvious than the words of the Bible that my father has just showed you?"

Robert replied, "If the words your father just showed me are translated correctly, then I certainly will have something to think about. But I have to see if the first century Greek actually says the words he just showed me."

The pastor balked. "Why would you even say something like that?"

"Because the words in your Bible say the identity of the Beast is a great mystery that will only be known to those with special insight — while the Greek Bible says the exact opposite; the Greek says only a crazy person won't be able to identify the Beast by the number of his name. And the words in your Bible say the Beast will be a future eighth 'king' — while the Greek simply doesn't say that. The Greek says that out of the seven kings, he is an eighth (a very popular first century expression, saying that the number of the Beast's name is a number associated with the eighth triangle unit). I'm not saying you're wrong, but at this point, I can no longer assume that you're right either. I have to check it out myself."

The pastor sat dumbfounded for a moment, then asked, "But how can you check it out? Where can anyone go to get a better answer than the one provided by the translators of the Bible itself?"

"I just have to check the Koine papyri. That's all," Robert replied.

"What's that?" the pastor responded.

"In the early 1900s, archaeologists discovered literally tons of

---

34 Revelation 13:8 NIV

early Greek manuscripts in the Egyptian desert — called the Koine papyri. Thanks to the Koine papyri, anyone can see how the Greek words were used in the first century — the time Jesus' disciples wrote the Bible. And now that we have literally tons of material (a veritable encyclopedia of information), we can have total confidence in the precise meaning of the common words used at this time."

"Well, I'm confident your research will show you why the translators of the Bible wrote the sentence the way they did."

Chapter 15

That afternoon, after Maria tried finishing her homework, she was still pondering the odd phone call she had just received. Why did Valerie feel compelled to keep up the running theological debate? Maria couldn't shake the thought that Valerie might have a hidden agenda. And it must involve her relationship with Robert.

The things Valerie had just told her were very unsettling. Maria told herself, "If I'm going to have an excuse to be near Robert, I need to be able to give Valerie a response."

Maria decided she had to see her pastor right away.

In the pastor's office, Maria entered and sat down. Shaking her head, she said, "According to Valerie, Jesus' disciples taught the first Christians that they're not under any law whatsoever. So she says it doesn't even matter that Jesus said the Golden Rule is the Law."

"You really should start attending Sunday School class before services," the pastor lightly chided.

Maria frowned. "I know," she said. "It's just that my shifts at the shelter end so late on Saturdays—."

"You volunteer on Saturdays *too*?" the pastor interrupted.

"Yes," Maria sighed.

"Tell you what," the pastor said, while rising from his chair. "Let me give you the Cliff Notes version of a Sunday School class I teach. I think you'll find it most helpful."

Maria sat up straight. "That'd be great. What's it about?"

"In class, we step back in time to discover 'Three First Century Christian Beliefs' held by Jesus' first Jewish followers," the pastor replied.

The pastor pulled some notes from his filing cabinet. Then he walked over and wiped clean a whiteboard. Then he wrote:

Three First Century Christian Beliefs

The pastor looked to Maria. "By the time we fill in this table, I believe you'll have the answer you were looking for."

"Ok," Maria replied. "Go for it."

The pastor dove right in. "'Love your neighbor as yourself' was considered the second greatest command in all the Jewish scriptures. And do you recall what Jewish books contained the official teachings which concur with each scripture?"

Maria hesitated. "Targums?"

The pastor nodded. "Let me show you the Targum teaching which concurs with the scripture, 'love your neighbor as yourself.'"

The pastor showed Maria the following:

Love your neighbor as yourself; **whatever you dislike do not do to him**.[35]

Then he explained. "First century Jews were taught that treating others the same way they want to be treated is the teaching which concurs with the scripture, 'Love your neighbor as yourself.' In other words, they were taught: *the Golden Rule is the teaching which concurs with the scripture, 'Love your neighbor as yourself.'*

The pastor wrote the first century Jewish Christian belief on the board.

---

35 *Leviticus Targum*, entry for Leviticus 19:18

Three First Century Christian Beliefs

The Golden Rule concurs with the scripture, "Love your neighbor as yourself."

The pastor continued. "The Babylonian version[36] of the Jewish Scriptures shows us another first century religious belief."

> Behold, My Servant, whom I uphold;
> My chosen one in whom My soul delights
> I have put My Spirit upon Him;
> He will bring forth justice to the nations.
> He will not be disheartened or crushed
> Until He has established justice in the earth;
> **And the coastlands will wait expectantly for His law.**"[37]

The pastor explained. "The Babylonian version of the Biblical book Isaiah (along with the Dead Sea Scrolls[38]) reveals that the Jews were waiting for the Messiah[39] — the King of Jews — to bring forth his Law."

The pastor added this first century Christian belief to the board.

---

36 For a complete discussion of the differences between the Babylonian version and the Egyptian version of the Jewish scriptures, please see *The Jerome Conspiracy*.

37 Isaiah 42:1, 4 NASB (A Bible which uses the Babylonian Version of the Jewish Scriptures)

38 Such as Dead Sea Scroll 4Q174

39 In the ancient Jewish nation, men became kings during an 'anointing ceremony' (see Samuel 2, for example). The Jewish nation was looking forward to a future king — a future 'anointed one' — to come and rule over them for an age, an age in which those who were faithful to God received the reward of enduring life while those who were unfaithful to God received punishment. *Messiah* is the Hebrew word for 'anointed one' (*Christ* is the equivalent in Greek). For the Jews, the title 'king' and 'Messiah' ('Christ') were interchangeable. They both referenced the prophesied future king — the prophesied coming of the anointed one.

> **Three First Century Christian Beliefs**
>
> The Golden Rule concurs with the scripture, "Love your neighbor as yourself."
>
> The Messiah — The King — will come and proclaim his Law.

Then the pastor pointed at the board. "With this in mind, think about what Jesus' first Jewish followers understood the moment he said:

Treat others the way you want to be treated **for this is the Law."**

Maria smiled. "Jesus proclaimed that the Golden Rule, which concurs with the scripture, 'Love your neighbor as yourself,' is his Law."

The pastor added this first century Christian belief to the board.

> **Three First Century Christian Beliefs**
>
> The Golden Rule concurs with the scripture, "Love your neighbor as yourself."
>
> The Messiah — The King — will come and proclaim his Law.
>
> Jesus declared that the Golden Rule, which concurs with the scripture, "Love your neighbor as yourself," is his Law.

With a completely blank look, Maria said, "And this is important because…"

The pastor explained further. "Maria, Jesus was the Messiah — the King. When Jesus said the Golden Rule is his Law, his followers understood that the Golden Rule is the Law of the Messiah — the King's Law. And they all understood that the King's Law (the Golden Rule) concurs with the scripture, 'Love your neighbor as yourself.'"

"I'm still not following you, Pastor," Maria sighed. "How does that answer my question on what his earliest followers taught their converts about the Law?"

The pastor opened his Greek Literal Bible. "Let me read you

something that should clear this up."

> If, however, you are fulfilling **the King's Law**[40] **which concurs with the scripture, "Love your neighbor as yourself,"** you are doing well. — James 2:8 Literal Greek

The light bulbs finally turned on. "So Jesus' apostles did teach their converts to follow a Law!" Maria exclaimed. "And not only that, they taught their converts to follow Jesus' Law — treat others the way you want to be treated — the Golden Rule!"

Maria was delighted that James had instructed his converts to follow the Golden Rule — the Law which concurs with the scripture, "Love your neighbor as yourself." She looked up at the poster: *Only one commandment, only one deciding factor - love one another.* "Did James also teach that the Golden Rule is going to be the deciding factor on Judgment Day?" she asked.

¤ ¤ ¤

Robert was in the reference section of the library, hunched over a copy of Moulton and Milligan's *Vocabulary of the Greek Testament* — the standard language reference work which catalogues the meaning of Greek words as they were used in the Koine papyri. Word-by-word, he checked the phrase, 'All the inhabitants of the earth will worship the Beast.' And when he got to the word translated as 'earth', he stopped dead in his tracks. Robert's heart skipped a beat before galloping ahead. For in the reference work, Robert read:

> It may be observed that the Greek word *ge* in papyri is regularly 'land' in small or moderate quantities, a sense never found in the NT, where *ge* is always antithetic to sky or sea, or **denotes a district or country**.[41]

---

40 Basilikon nomon = 'the King's Law.'

In archaeology: 'Basilikon nomon' was found in a first century inscription in Pergamum, written during the reign of Trajan. The inscription describes royal laws as being Laws made by the King himself.

In literature: 1 Esdras 8:24 KJV (basilikon nomon = 'the law of the King'); 2 Maccabees 3:13 KJV (basilikas entolas = 'the King's commandment')

41 *Vocabulary of the Greek Testament*, J.H. Moulton and G. Milligan, p.125

Robert was furious. "The Koine Greek isn't necessarily talking about someone who will be worshiped by the entire earth," he said to himself. "The Koine Greek can simply be referring to someone who was worshiped by the districts in the lands. And of course, there were first century leaders who were worshipped in their lands. That happened many times in the distant past. The passage doesn't require a yet future Beast of Revelation like Valerie's dad says it does, not even in the slightest."

Robert added this newfound information to the clues regarding the identity of the Beast of Revelation:

CLUES TO THE BEAST OF REVELATION:

The number of the beast's name is 666, which means the sum of the symbols of his name is 666.

Anybody with half a brain will know him by this number, which means the beast was so popular that only a crazy person wouldn't recognize him by the number 666.

Out of the seven kings, he is an eighth, which means there is a list of seven kings, and the one whose name is 666 (an eighth), is the Beast.

All the inhabitants of the country worship him, which means he is a king who was worshiped as a deity by the inhabitants of his land.

Chapter 16

The pastor leaned back in his chair and looked Maria intently in the eyes. "Do you have any idea how revolutionary Jesus' Law was?" he asked. "When Jesus said, 'Treat everyone the same way you want to be treated, *for this is the Law*,' he turned the first century religious world upside down."

"How so?" Maria asked.

"The Jews were convinced that they must follow every nitty gritty detail of Moses' Law in order to be on the narrow road to life. And the Law of Moses was tough, very tough. For instance, the Law of Moses restricted what people could eat, down to the detail of even forbidding the consumption of shellfish.[42] But according to Jesus' Law, what people eat doesn't matter. Jesus' Law freed them from a slew of dietary rules and regulations.

"The Law of Moses also severely restricted what people could wear, down to the detail of even forbidding the use of garments made of two or more fabrics.[43] But according to Jesus' Law, what people wear doesn't matter. Jesus' Law freed them from a slew of clothing rules and regulations.

"The Law of Moses also severely restricted when people could work, down to the detail of even demanding that a person be stoned to death simply for gathering firewood to keep his family warm on the Sabbath.[44] But according to Jesus' Law, Sabbath observation and limitations on work don't matter. Jesus' Law freed them from a slew of Sabbath and work-related rules and regulations.

"In a very direct way, when Jesus declared, 'Treat others the way you want to be treated, for this is the Law,' Jesus issued *the Law that gives freedom*: freedom from food restrictions, freedom from clothing restrictions, freedom from work restrictions, freedom from Sabbath restrictions, and freedom from much, much more. The Golden Rule

---

42 Leviticus 11:10-12
43 Leviticus 19:19
44 Numbers 15:32-36; Exodus 35:3

is *the Law that gives freedom* from thousands of religious rules and regulations."

"Interesting," Maria remarked. "But why are you telling me this?"

"Because," the pastor replied, "you asked if James ever wrote that the Golden Rule — the Law that gives freedom — is going to be the deciding factor on Judgment Day."

The pastor opened his Bible to the book of James and read:

> Speak and act as **those who are going to be judged by the law that gives freedom.**[45]

"So James did teach that the Golden Rule — the Law that gives freedom — will be the deciding factor on Judgment Day," Maria said with a smile.

Maria looked back at the poster: *Only one commandment, only one deciding factor — love one another.*

"I finally get your poster now!" she exclaimed. "The Golden Rule has only one commandment. The Golden Rule is the one deciding factor on Judgment Day. And the Golden Rule is fulfilled when we love one another. So when Jesus said the Golden Rule was his Law, he was teaching, 'There is *only one commandment, only one deciding factor — love one another.*'"

According to the Book of Matthew:

Treating others the way you want them to treat you is the Law.

Those who do this are on the narrow road that leads to life.

Those who do not do this are on the broad road that leads to destruction.

In other words, according to the book of Matthew, *there is only one commandment, only one deciding factor — love one another.*

According to the Book of John:

---

45 James 2:12 NIV

Those who abide in Jesus (by following his commandments) will have life.

Those who do not abide in Jesus (by not following his commandments) will be thrown into the fire.

Jesus has only one commandment: love one another.

In other words, according to the book of John, *there is only one commandment, only one deciding factor — love one another.*

According to the book of 1st John:

This is God's commandment: to trust the Son enough to love one another just as he commanded.

By loving others, we know we have passed from death to life.

For it is those who do not love others who remain in death.

In other words, according to 1st John, *there is only one commandment, only one deciding factor — love one another.*

According to the Book of James:

The King's Law concurs with the scripture, "Love your neighbor as yourself." (In other words, the King's Law is the Golden Rule — the Jewish Targum teaching that concurs with the scripture, "Love your neighbor as yourself.")

Those who fulfill the King's Law — the Golden Rule — are doing well.

For everyone will be judged by the Golden Rule — this law which brings freedom from all the meaningless religious rules and regulations.

Therefore, according to James' letter, *there is only one commandment, only one deciding factor — love one another.*

Chapter 17

Maria thought about the implications of the Golden Rule. "Pastor, I have a favor to ask you."

"What is it?"

Maria hadn't stopped worrying about the waitress, Patricia, and her dilemma. At least her concern for the woman had — for the moment — allowed her to compartmentalize her longing to be with Robert. Here was a woman whose problems were clearly more pressing than her own.

"There's a waitress at Sammy's who has a young son with a very serious medical condition — one she fears could even take his life. But she can't get any doctors to look at him, because she has no money and no insurance. Do you think any of the doctors who attend our church might be willing to help her?"

¤ ¤ ¤

Robert lay facing up in his dorm room, staring vaguely, pondering to himself. "Valerie's Bible says only those with special insight will know who the Beast is; yet the actual Bible says only a crazy person won't know who he is.

"Valerie's church teaches that the 666 number of the Beast's name is an unknowable riddle; yet identifying people by the numbers of their name was a very common — therefore knowable — first century convention.

"Valerie's Bible says the Beast will be worshiped by the entire world; yet the actual Bible doesn't specify 'the entire world' — a person worshiped by a district or country would totally fulfill the description.

"And Valerie's Bible says the Beast will be a future eighth king; yet the actual Bible says that out of seven kings, he is an eighth — meaning his identity is related to the eighth triangular unit (which 666 already shows, anyway).

69

"I want to discuss what I've just discovered with Valerie, but I'm not sure she's the best source of information anymore.... I just don't know what to do."

Robert closed his eyes. "Mom, I wish you were here to help me."

Instantly, Robert lit up, goose bumps dancing on his arms. "Of course! I know how to figure out who the Beast is. All I have to do is figure out who the seven kings are — and find out which of them matches the description."

Robert opened his Greek Bible to Revelation, and read chapters thirteen through seventeen. He stopped the moment he read:

> The seven heads are seven hills on which the woman sits. They are also seven kings.[46]

"Of course, only an imbecile wouldn't know who the seven kings are. It's right here ... plain as day!" Robert was brimming with excitement. He grabbed the clues to the Beast, thought for just a second, and then shouted, "And I know which one is the Beast! Now I know why only a first century imbecile wouldn't know who he is, as well!"

¤ ¤ ¤

Maria told Valerie how the Aramaic Targums reveal that the Golden Rule is the Jewish principle which concurs with the scripture, "Love your neighbor as yourself." And she further explained that James had instructed his converts to follow the King's Law, which concurs with the scripture, "Love your neighbor as yourself" — a direct reference to Jesus' statement that the Golden Rule is his Law.

Maria further explained how defining the entire Law by the Golden Rule brought freedom from thousands of rules and regulations — it was truly 'the Law that gives freedom.' She then shared with Valerie how James wrote that Christians will be judged by the Golden Rule — the Law that gives freedom.

"Really?" Valerie scoffed. "So none of *Paul's* writings matter to your pastor?"

---

46 Revelation 17:9

Maria was taken aback. "What do you mean?"

Valerie explained. "James wrote only one book in the entire Bible. It was the apostle Paul who wrote more books of the Bible than anyone else. And even though Paul wasn't one of Jesus's disciples — nor did he ever meet Jesus personally — he was the one who wrote the theology that Christianity is based upon."

Maria was speechless.

Valerie continued. "So let me show you what Paul wrote in a letter to the Christians in the city of Galatia in one of my favorite Bible passages."

Valerie read the following:

> Nevertheless knowing that a **man is not justified by the works of the Law but through faith** in Christ Jesus, even we have believed in Christ Jesus, so that we may be justified by faith in Christ and **not by the works of the Law**; since **by the works of the Law no flesh will be justified**. [47]

Then she triumphantly declared, "James' letter must be read in light of the numerous writings of Paul. And Paul's letter to the Galatians makes it clear that Christians are saved by their faith — apart from any law whatsoever. In fact, the words Paul wrote are so plain and simple that it's beyond me why your pastor refuses to accept them."

¤ ¤ ¤

Patricia was still completely stunned by the act of kindness from the woman in the restaurant who had caused her to spill her tray. Maria had made arrangements for her to see Dr. Corbin, a doctor whom she said belongs to her church. Her little boy Jack would be seen by the best doctor in the city — and Patricia would not have to worry about paying a penny. The only thing that Patricia had to do was show up at his office for the appointment.

Patricia explained her son's symptoms to the doctor — the breathlessness, especially when exerting himself, the swelling of his ankles and feet, the fatigue, the irregular heartbeats, the light headedness, and the most concerning of all — the fainting. Then the nurse took Jack back to the reception room.

"Sounds like a classic case of cardiomyopathy," the doctor told

---

47 Galatians 2:16

Patricia.

"Is it serious?"

Dr. Corbin paused for a moment, then said softly, "It all depends on the type and severity."

"What do you mean, *type*?"

"There are three types of cardiomyopathy, but without further tests, I wouldn't want to speculate as to which one he has."

Patricia was both relieved for finally getting a diagnosis, yet fearful for what lay ahead for her little boy. "I'm begging you, Doctor. Please … I need as much information as I can get."

After a moment, Dr. Corbin conceded. "Well, one type is very rare, so it's probably not that one. And one type tends to affect people only when they're middle-aged — so it's also not likely to be the one. But the third type, hypertrophic cardiomyopathy, can occur at any age."

"OK," Patricia said. She paused for a moment, unable to utter the question. Then she looked at the doctor with watery eyes and asked, "Can this type of cardiomyopathy kill my son?"

The doctor remained silent.

A tear fell from Patricia's face. "Doctor, please answer my question. Can it be fatal?"

Dr. Corbin placed his hand on Patricia's shoulder. "Depending on the severity… yes. But at this point, let's hope for the best."

¤ ¤ ¤

Every time the telephone rang, Patricia jumped. Three days after the appointment with the doctor, she finally received a call from the nurse at the doctor's office. She waited for what seemed like an eternity for the nurse to get Dr. Corbin onto the phone.

"I'm afraid that he has an unusually advanced stage of the disease, for a young boy," the doctor said in a somber tone. "The test results have confirmed that your son does have hypertrophic cardiomyopathy. If he's not treated right away, the prognosis is very poor. I've already contacted a cardiologist from the church and he has agreed to take on your son's case for free. And he's already arranged for the hospital to classify your son's condition as life-threatening, so the hospital will basically supply its services at cost, which will reduce your portion of the bill for surgery and care from around $70,000 to about $30,000."

Patricia was overwhelmed by a mix of emotions: relief and gratitude, but numbed by the figure she had just heard. "I appreciate all that you've done, Dr. Corbin. But I don't have the $30,000. Is there any other alternative?"

"I'm very sorry, Patricia. But that's the best I'm able to do."

After she hung up the phone, Patricia finally broke down. Looking toward heaven, she said, "I thought this was going to be my miracle. Why have you turned your back on my son?"

Chapter 18

Maria was beginning to feel as if she were wearing her welcome out at her pastor's office. But the pastor always welcomed her warmly, applauding her interest in the Bible.

"Welcome back," the pastor chuckled when he saw Maria in the doorway.

"Hi Pastor," she said, while taking a seat. "I'm so sorry to keep bothering you."

"Bothering me? ... You have no idea how delighted I am that you're finally taking a strong interest in the Bible. ... Not that I've ever worried about your soul. You do so much volunteering for the nursing home and the food shelter that I've always known your heart is with God, but it still makes me glad to see your newfound interest in the Bible."

Maria once again launched right in. "Valerie showed me that, in Paul's letter to the Christians in Galatia, he wrote that people 'are not justified by the works of the Law.'"

"Paul wrote that people are not justified by the works of *which* Law, Maria?" the pastor calmly asked.

Maria simply stared at the pastor with a befuddled look upon her face.

The pastor continued. "Did Paul say that people aren't justified by the Law of Moses or the Law of the Messiah — the King's Law?"

Chapter 19

"Why the hell do you keep bothering me?" Jack Sr. growled over the phone line.

Patricia was shaking so badly that she thought she was going to drop the phone.

Before she could say another word, Jack barked, "I should've changed my number the day I left. I never thought you'd call to bother me so much."

Patricia took a deep breath and almost blurted the words out. "Our son needs an operation to save his life, and it'll cost $30,000. I know you've put some money away. And I'm not asking you to give it to me. I'm just asking to borrow it. I'll pay you back with interest. I swear."

Patricia's answer was the click of Jack's phone hanging up.

¤ ¤ ¤

The pastor explained. "Maria, the entire New Testament is a contrast of two Laws: the Law of Moses and the Law of the Messiah — the King's Law. This includes Paul's letter to the Galatians. And you can easily prove this to Valerie."

The pastor read the following:

> What I am saying is this: **the Law, which came four hundred and thirty years later**, doesn't nullify a covenant previously established by God, so as to break the promise.[48]

> Bear one another's burdens and so fulfill **the Law of the Messiah**.[49]

The pastor explained. "First show Valerie that Paul's letter to the Galatians discusses two different Laws: the Law which came four

---

48 Galatians Chapter Three
49 Galatians Chapter Six

hundred and thirty years later (the Law of Moses) and the Law of the
Messiah — the King's Law. After she understands that Paul discusses
two very different Laws, simply show her what Paul wrote about each
of these Laws."

The pastor read the following.

> Nevertheless knowing that **a man is not justified by the works of the Law...**
> What I am saying is this: **the Law, which came four hundred and thirty
> years later**, does not invalidate a covenant previously ratified by God, so as
> to nullify the promise.[50]

> Bear one another's burdens and so fulfill **the Law of the Messiah....** Let
> us not give up on doing good, for **in due time we will reap if we do not get
> tired. So then, while we have the chance, let us be helpful to everyone.**[51]

The pastor explained. "Paul's letter to the Galatians is actually
simple. When speaking about the Law of Moses, he said that no one
will be justified by this Law. When speaking of the Law of the Messiah
— the King's Law — he said they must not tire in bearing the burdens
of others (they must not tire of following the Messiah's Law) if they
want to reap the reward. One Law doesn't justify, while following the
other is absolutely essential."

Maria looked up at the poster: *Only one commandment, only
one deciding factor - love one another.* "I never knew that phrase you
have us recite every Sunday ran throughout the Bible like that."

---

50   Galatians 2:16, 3:17 NASB
51   Galatians 6:2, 9-10 Literal Greek

Chapter 20

Using every ounce of determination she could muster, Patricia walked into Sammy's.

The manager came straight to her. "You're not supposed to be here for a couple more hours," he said.

"I know," Patricia responded. "I'm here to talk to you."

"What about?"

"My son needs an operation and I need to save money. I need extra shifts."

"You know you're already on thin ice."

Patricia bowed her head. "Yes, I know."

"I know I'll probably regret this, but I just fired a waitress not five minutes ago. I'll let you have her shifts. On one condition."

"Anything."

"If you're late, even by one minute, don't even bother coming in, because you won't have any shifts here at all. Got it?"

"Yes, sir. You won't regret it. I promise."

¤ ¤ ¤

Maria could hardly wait to tell Valerie about what she had just learned.

"I'm not wasting any more energy with you on this," Valerie said on the phone, before Maria even had a chance to begin. "If you haven't accepted the truth by now, I doubt you ever will. I'd rather spend my time with people who really want to learn." Then she hung up.

Maria felt as if she had been punched hard in the stomach. "Oh my God! Now I've lost my last connection to Robert."

Completely lost as to what to do next, all she could manage was to bury her head under her pillow and sob.

Chapter 21

Robert pulled Valerie through the doorway into his dorm room and — without so much as a "Hello" — launched into telling her about his inspired analysis of Revelation. "As soon as I read, 'The seven heads are seven hills on which the woman sits. They are also seven kings,' I immediately realized who the seven kings are — just like any first century reader would have."

"Oh, you did?" Valerie said, unconvinced.

"In the first century, the 'seven hills' — which were mentioned in numerous writings — always referred to one place and one place only — Rome. For example, take a look at this passage from a first century Christian writing."

> Among most men, and robbery of temples.
> And then shall, after these, appear of men
> The tenth race, when the earth-shaking Lightener
> Shall break the zeal for idols and shall shake
> The people of **seven-hilled Rome**, and riches great.[52]

Robert further explained. "Rome, the very center of first century civilization, was so commonly known as the City of Seven Hills, that authors often used the phrase as a euphemism for the city itself. So every first century reader would have instantly thought of Rome the moment they read 'the seven heads are seven hills.'"

"Go on," Valerie said

"Therefore, the seven kings have to be *the first seven emperors of Rome*. In Greek writings, the Greek word 'king' was used for the Roman emperors.[53] And Revelation says, 'five kings have fallen, one is, and one is yet to come.' And if only five kings have fallen, then Revelation is specifically talking about the first seven kings — not any

---

52 Sibylline Oracles, Book II, verse 15
53 An example from the Bible: "So they cried out, 'Away with Him, away with Him, crucify Him!' Pilate said to them, 'Shall I crucify your King?' The chief priests answered, '**We have no king but Caesar.**'" — John 19:15 NASB

other set of seven Roman kings."

"I'm following you so far."

Robert continued. "Therefore, I realized that the book of Revelation was calling one of the first seven emperors 'the Beast'. And then I remembered that Revelation also says the Beast is worshipped by the inhabitants of the land, which allowed me to narrow the possibilities down to two of the kings."

"Which two?"

"Out of the first seven kings of Rome, only two of them received worship while they were alive: Caligula and Nero. So I realized that Revelation has to be referring to one of them. So I had to look for a piece of information in Revelation that could apply only to Caligula, or only to Nero, to know for sure who the Beast is."

"So what did you find?"

He opened his Bible and said, "The final piece of the puzzle was found in this passage from Revelation."

Valerie read;

> There was given to him a mouth speaking arrogant words and blasphemies, **and authority to act for forty-two months was given to him.** And he opened his mouth in blasphemies against God, to blaspheme His name and His tabernacle, that is, those who dwell in heaven. **It was also given to him to make war with the saints and to overcome them.**[54]

Robert explained. "Nero made war against the Christians starting in the middle of November in 64 AD — shortly after a fire that he started in Rome and then blamed on the Christians. And Nero never ceased persecuting the Christians up until his death in 68 AD — 42 months later."[55]

"I never realized Nero waged a war against the Christians for forty-two months. That does seem to be more than just a coincidence."

"Of course!" Robert triumphantly declared.

Valerie gulped. "And I assume you're going to tell me that the number of Nero's name is 666?" she asked.

"Well, it must be," Robert answered.

"You mean you haven't checked it out?"

Robert shook his head. "The other clues are so solid. I just

---

54   Revelation 13:5-7
55   *The Beast of Revelation*, Dr. Kenneth Gentry Jr., Chapter 5, Copyright 2002

assumed that the number of Nero's name must be 666."

"But Robert," Valerie exclaimed, "the number 666 is the most important part of identifying the Beast. You yourself said that it's the number 666 that would allow any first century reader to know the identity of the Beast."

"So let's do it right now. I've got all the symbols here in my notes from class."

Robert wrote Nero's name in Greek symbols then added them together — producing the number of Nero's name according to the very common first century convention. All the color drained from his face when he saw the number. "No!" he said. "This can't be right!"

Valerie smiled. "What did you find?"

Robert showed Valerie the number of Nero's name in Greek: 1,332.

"So Nero isn't the Beast!" she chirped.

Robert sat stunned for a moment, before inspiration hit. "Ah! But Revelation was written to the first Christian converts. The twelve apostles spent their lives converting Jews — only the apostle Paul focused on converting non-Jews. So Revelation was likely written exclusively to Jewish congregations (since it wasn't written by Paul), and the Jewish recipients would be fluent in Hebrew."

"So?" Valerie interjected.

"So perhaps the number of Nero's name in Hebrew is 666."

Robert wrote out Nero's name in Hebrew and summed the symbols together. After he read the sum, he ripped the piece of paper to shreds.

"I assume the number isn't 666 in Hebrew, either."

"No, it's not," Robert said, dejected. "The number of Nero's Hebrew name is 616."

Valerie was all aglow. "So Nero isn't the Beast. And therefore, my church must be correct that the Beast will be someone in the future, who will be identified by the number 666, right?"

Chapter 22

Patricia stood at the hall mirror, putting on the last touches of makeup before work. She grabbed her house keys, gave Jack a kiss on the forehead, and walked to the door. As she reached for the doorknob, she heard something behind her. She turned and saw that Jack had collapsed, out cold.

She rushed to his side and shook him. The little boy regained consciousness a few seconds later. Patricia held him tightly.

Patricia stayed with her son, waiting for him to become stable. After she saw that he had fully recovered, she looked up at the clock. "Oh my God, I'm going to be so late."

¤ ¤ ¤

Robert was confused and disappointed that the number of Nero's name in neither Greek nor Hebrew added up to 666.

Valerie pressed. "You do realize that you have to let go of this Nero theory of yours."

Robert remained silent.

"You realize that the number 666 is by far the most important key to identifying the Beast," Valerie told him. "After all, the book of Revelation applies the number 666 to even more than just the name of the Beast."

"What do you mean?"

Valerie showed Robert the following passage from Revelation:

> **He made it so that no one is able to buy or to sell, except the one who has the mark: either the name of the Beast or the number of his name.** And here is the sacred information: Let anyone with the mind calculate the number of the Beast, **for the number is that of a man; and his number is six hundred and sixty-six.**[56]

---

56 Revelation 13:17-18

Then she explained. "The Bible not only says the number 666 is the number of the Beast's name, but it also says that people will use that number for buying and selling. Has there ever been a time in history when people used the number 666 when buying and selling?"

After a few moments of thinking about her question, Robert had to acknowledge Valerie's logic. "No, there hasn't been. I'm sorry for doubting you and your father. I can see I need to start listening to experts like you and your dad. Can you accept my apology?"

"Of course!" Valerie quickly offered. "I love your passion for the Bible."

Robert took out the piece of paper where he was keeping track of the clues to the Beast of Revelation and he ripped it to shreds. "That's it. I'm done. The number 666 clearly has nothing to do with Nero's name — and it certainly doesn't have anything to do with buying or selling at any point in history. I was foolish not to believe you. And I won't second guess you anymore."

"Thank you," Valerie replied, before giving Robert a hug. "You don't know how glad I am that we can move beyond this. I've been hoping that, after you've learned more about Bible prophecy, you might want to think about joining me on my missionary trip. But I'm going to need your answer very soon, because there's only one slot available and I've asked the director of the trip to keep it open — for you — if you're interested."

Chapter 23

Patricia walked into Sammy's — one hour late.

Her boss made a beeline for her. "Go home," he said, pointing to the door.

"It'll never happen again, I promise."

"You're right. It'll never happen again, because you no longer work here."

The manager turned, walked into his office, and closed the door.

Patricia stepped outside the restaurant, pressed her back up against the concrete wall, and broke down.

¤ ¤ ¤

Robert couldn't shake Valerie's invitation off his mind. Not just the amazing opportunity, but also the fact that it was clear to him that her interest went beyond being strictly 'missionary buddies'.

Maybe it's finally time to move on, Robert thought to himself. *After all, Maria hasn't budged one bit. It's not like I haven't given her several chances.*

He also couldn't help but think of his mother and what her thoughts would be. His mother would have been much happier seeing him with Valerie than Maria.

Try as he did, however, to tell himself that there was no hope for them, he just couldn't make that final mental break. Perhaps he should give her one final chance — to see if there was any possible hope of reconciliation. And to save her from being left behind at the Rapture. He owed it to her, the woman who had been the love of his life for so long. He picked up the phone and dialed.

"Robert!" Maria answered.

"I was calling to see how your conversations have been going with Valerie. She doesn't tell me much about what you guys talk about."

"I'm sure she doesn't," Maria answered.

"What do you mean?"

"The more I talk to Valerie, the more I'm convinced that being a Christian is totally about helping others out, not about this 'salvation by faith' nonsense."

"But Christianity is about the spiritual world, not the earthly one. The earth is temporary. Heaven is forever."

"You've got the Bible backwards, Robert," Maria said. "The Bible is all about making life here on earth better for our fellow man in exchange for God granting us a better life in the next."

Robert balked. "After all this time with Valerie, you only sound more convinced of your church's teachings!"

"Yes! And I'd love to tell you why. I think I've learned enough to show you that Valerie isn't following the Bible at all."

Robert felt tears welling in his eyes. "The real reason for this call was to see if there was any hope of us reconciling. And now I see that we've only grown further apart. I've learned not to question Valerie and her father. I've learned that they know so much more than me, and I won't question them any longer. Goodbye, Maria. I can't tell you how much this hurts me."

Robert hung up the phone without waiting for a response.

¤ ¤ ¤

Patricia stood outside the apartment manager's door and said a silent prayer before she knocked.

The manager opened the door. "What do you want?"

Patricia replied as sweetly as she possibly could. "I just want to let you know that I might need a few extra days to make rent this month. But I promise, I'll get it to you as fast as I can."

"Do you know how many applications I have for an apartment like yours? Applications from people who will pay me on time?"

"Please let me explain —," Patricia began.

But the manager interrupted her. "Listen, we've all got problems. And if you're late, then I've got a problem. The rules are simple. Either pay on time or get out. Got it?"

Chapter 24

"I'm calling to let you know that I'm seriously thinking about going with you on that missionary trip." Robert could hear the excitement in Valerie's voice as she told him how wonderful she thought that was. Then he said, "And I'm also calling to ask a very big favor of you."

"Sure!"

"Would you please try one more time to get through to Maria? Can you take some extra time to prepare your best possible presentation on where her church is wrong? And if Maria doesn't budge after you've given it your all — then I'll know there's no hope. Then I'll know it's time for me to finally let go completely. Will you help me?"

¤ ¤ ¤

Valerie said a prayer the moment she hung up the phone. "Dear Heavenly Father, I really need your guidance right now. If it's possible for Maria to be saved, if there's anything I can do to get through to her, I need you to show me the way. I'm putting this whole situation in your hands and I trust you to work this out for your glory. In Jesus' name, Amen."

¤ ¤ ¤

When the two young women sat down at the booth at Sammy's, Maria noticed Valerie had brought some papers with her this time.

Valerie started. "I prayed and asked God for guidance on what to share with you. And God pressed on my heart that I should tell the history of how the doctrine of 'salvation by faith' was discovered. So I prepared a short presentation for you."

"Of course I'm open to listening to whatever you feel God wants you to share."

Valerie explained. "A sixteenth century German Monk named

Martin Luther is often called 'the father of Protestantism'. And just like you, he belonged to a church system that taught that salvation depends on our actions. I'm praying that once you learn what opened his eyes to 'salvation by faith', it'll open your own eyes as well."

"I'm still listening," Maria affirmed.

Valerie continued. "Martin Luther discovered 'salvation by faith' when he was reading the Biblical book of Romans — one of the Apostle Paul's letters that are in the Bible."

Valerie handed Maria a paper with the following:

> **This discovery [of salvation by faith] is often called Luther's "Tower Experience,"** because in one of his **"table talks"** he mentions that he was studying <u>Romans 1:17</u> in the heated room (his study) of the tower of the **Black Cloister in Wittenberg when the light broke upon him**….

> **Luther makes it clear in several places that this, not the Theses, was the pivotal event of his life.** The most important of these appears in his Preface to the Complete Edition of Luther's Latin Writings of 1545. Several other mentions of the event are recorded from his "Table Talks," one from 1532 (LW 54:193-194), one from 1538 (LW 54:308-309), and one from 1542-43 (LW 54:442-443). [57]

Then Valerie explained. "Martin Luther stated many times that it was Romans 1:17 that opened his eyes to salvation by faith. In fact, Martin Luther wrote that this particular sentence in Romans 1:17 was pivotal to his epiphany."

Valerie showed Maria the following:

The righteous shall live by **faith**. — Romans 1:17

"In this sentence, Paul (the author of Romans) was quoting the prophet Habakkuk. More specifically, Paul was quoting Habakkuk 2:4. And it was Paul's quote of Habakkuk 2:4 that opened Martin Luther's eyes."

"But didn't Martin Luther's church leaders know about Paul's quote of Habakkuk 2:4?" Maria asked.

Valerie nodded. "Yes, they did. But they taught Martin Luther the wrong meaning of it," she said. "You see, in Greek, Paul wrote:

The righteous shall live by *pistis*.

---

57   From "Martin Luther's Tower Experience," article by Dr. Richard P. Bucher

"And Martin Luther's teachers told him that *pistis* meant 'faithfulness'. They told Martin Luther that Paul's letter was discussing active righteousness[58] — *faithfulness* to righteous deeds. But Martin Luther knew they were wrong. After all, he was a Greek scholar himself. And he knew Paul's quote of Habakkuk 2:4 was really discussing salvation by faith, not faithfulness. And the moment Martin Luther realized his teachers had taught him wrongly about Paul's quote of Habakkuk 2:4 (in his 'Tower Experience'), his life changed forever. And he lit the torch of the Protestant Reformation — he lit the torch of 'salvation by faith.'"

Maria folded her arms. "So Martin Luther went rogue. Big deal. How can you be so sure that he was right and all his religious teachers were wrong?"

"Huh?" Valerie gasped. "Think about it, Maria. This all happened four hundred years ago. And over the last four hundred years, one scholar after another has analyzed Martin Luther's discovery, and they have all concluded that he was right. It's your pastor who is 'going rogue'. You trust what your pastor has to say *against four hundred years of scholarship*. The weight of history and scholarship are squarely stacked up against you and your pastor, not against Martin Luther — not against me."

Maria gulped.

Valerie waited.

After a couple minutes, Maria spoke. "You sure have given me a lot to think about. I never knew four hundred years of scholarship has concluded that 'the righteous shall live by *pistis*', meaning that 'the righteous shall live by *faith*'. So I don't know why my pastor teaches us something so very different."

"Okay," said Valerie. "So are you going to trust four hundred years of experts, or a heretic?"

---

58 *Luther's Works* Volume 34, Career of the Reformer IV (St. Louis, Concordia Publishing House, 1960), p. 336-337

Chapter 25

Patricia entered her apartment at 8:00 at night, plopped herself down in the chair, took off her shoes, and massaged her feet. As she looked to heaven, she said, "God, *please.* I've been pounding the pavement looking for work, morning to night, all week, and nothing — absolutely nothing. Ever since I've asked for your help, things have only gotten much worse: my son is sicker, I lost my job, and soon — if you don't help me get a job — I'm going to lose my house, too. I don't mind you turning your back on me, but why have you abandoned my boy?"

¤ ¤ ¤

Maria opened the door, entered, and found her uncle, Dr. Richmond, grading papers. "Uncle Donny, I've never been so confused in my life. I really need your help."

Dr. Richmond motioned to the chair next to him. "What's wrong?"

"I'm starting to think that I might have lost Robert for all the wrong reasons. It has to do with religious history. And since you're a religious history professor, I'm hoping you can help me sort through everything."

"I'd be glad to try," her uncle offered.

Maria explained. "My pastor seems to use the Bible to defend our church's teachings very well. But Valerie showed me something I never realized. She showed me that Martin Luther's discovery of 'salvation by faith' from Paul's quote of Habakkuk 2:4 was the very foundation of the Protestant Reformation. And she also showed me that four hundred years of Biblical scholarship afterwards has continued to confirm that Paul's quote of Habakkuk 2:4 does teach that salvation is by faith — just like Martin Luther, the father of the Protestant Reformation, said. And when I think of how many Biblical scholars must have examined this over a period of four hundred years,

I can't help but question whether my pastor is way off base."

"And you learned all this history from Valerie?"

"Yes. She's the daughter of a pastor, and she's a theology major, and she's a missionary — I have to believe that she knows what she's talking about. In fact, she seems to even know some Greek too. She showed me that Paul's quote of Habakkuk 2:4 — 'the righteous shall live by *pistis*' — means that 'the righteous shall live by faith.' And she told me that numerous scholars over the last four hundred years have concluded that Martin Luther was right. So, Uncle Donny, does the Greek word *pistis* mean 'faith'?"

Dr. Richmond nodded. "Yes, *pistis* does indeed mean 'faith.'"

Maria's shoulders began to sag.

"And it also means 'faithfulness' and 'pledge' as well," Dr. Richmond quickly interjected.

"Huh?" Maria gasped.

"The Koine Greek word *pistis* had many meanings," her uncle replied.

Maria hung her head. "So we can never know which is the correct translation if the word has so many different meanings."

Dr. Richmond's head snapped back. "I'm not saying that *at all.*"

Maria's uncle walked up to the whiteboard and wrote:

The sailor drank the <u>port</u> while standing on the <u>port</u> of the ship which was docked at the <u>port</u>.

Then he explained. "The English word 'port' also has many meanings. Yet Maria, tell me, what is the one meaning of the first instance of 'port' in the sentence above?"

"Wine," Maria replied.

"And *how do you know*?" her uncle asked.

"Because the sailor is drinking the port; therefore, this 'port' has to be 'wine,'" she replied.

Her uncle nodded. "And Maria, what is the one meaning of the second instance of port?" he asked.

"The left side of the ship," Maria replied.

"And *how do you know*?" her uncle asked.

"Because the sailor is standing on some part of the ship; therefore, this 'port' has to be 'the left side of the ship,'" she replied.

Her uncle nodded once again. "And finally, Maria, what is the one meaning of the third instance of port?" he asked.

"The harbor," Maria replied.

"And *how do you know*?" her uncle asked.

"Because the ship is docked at this 'port'; therefore, this 'port' has to be 'the harbor,'" Maria replied.

Her uncle nodded yet again. "So you see, you can often know, with 100% certainty, what a word means by looking at the context in which it is mentioned."

Dr. Richmond wrote underneath the sentence:

> *The sailor drank the <u>wine</u> while standing on the <u>left side of the ship</u> which was docked at the <u>harbor</u>.*

"Once you know the context, you instantly know the correct meaning of the word," Dr. Richmond explained.

"Your example shows me this is true," Maria concurred. "So what was the topic of Habakkuk 2:4? And does the topic of Habakkuk 2:4 show *pistis* meant 'faith' or 'faithfulness'?

"It all depends on which version of Habakkuk 2:4 you're talking about," her uncle answered.

"Huh?"

Dr. Richmond explained. "Only quite recently were the contents of the Dead Sea Scrolls from cave four made public. And the contents of this cave have caused a firestorm in Biblical scholarship circles, because the contents document that there were two different versions of the Jewish scriptures: an Egyptian version and a Babylonian one. And are you ready for a big surprise?"

"I think so."

"The topic of the Egyptian Habakkuk 2:4 is entirely different than the topic of the Babylonian Habakkuk 2:4," Dr. Richmond revealed. "The Egyptian Habakkuk 2:4 discusses the necessity of *faithfulness to the coming Messiah*. However, the Babylonian version discusses the necessity of *steadfast trust to a coming message*.[59]"

"Okay," Maria interjected.

Dr. Richmond continued. "Jesus, his disciples and the early church all used the Egyptian version of the Jewish scriptures. When

---

59 Compare Habakkuk 2:4 LXX (Egyptian Version) to Habakkuk 2:4 NASB (Babylonian Version).

Paul wrote the book of Romans, he quoted the Egyptian version of Habakkuk 2:4 to remind his readers that they must remain *faithful to the Messiah*."

"Sounds pretty cut and dry," Maria remarked.

But her uncle shook his head from side to side. "Unfortunately, the plot thickens. The Egyptian version of the Jewish scriptures was used by the early church up until the fifth century. Then in the fifth century, a man named Jerome was given the task of translating the Bible into Latin. And he replaced the Egyptian version of the Jewish Scriptures with the Babylonian one.[60] The Babylonian version of the Jewish scriptures has been used in Christian Bibles ever since."

Dr. Richmond wrote out the following timeline:

First Century Bibles contain the Egyptian version of Habakkuk 2:4 — Paul quotes Habakkuk 2:4 to remind his readers they need to remain faithful to the Messiah.

Fifth Century Bible has replaced the Egyptian version with the Babylonian one — The topic of Habakkuk 2:4 has been changed. 'Faithfulness to the Messiah' has been replaced with 'steadfastness to a message'.

Sixteenth Century Bibles still contain the Babylonian version — Martin Luther reads Habakkuk 2:4 (which now speaks of steadfast trust in a message) and concludes that salvation is by 'faith in the Gospel'. (Martin Luther is totally unaware that Paul's Bible had a very different version of Habakkuk 2:4.)

For the next four hundred years, Bibles continue to contain the Babylonian Version — Since Bibles still contain the Babylonian version of Habakkuk 2:4, scholars conclude that Martin Luther is correct. (They also are unaware that Paul had a different version of Habakkuk 2:4.)

Maria was taken aback. "But doesn't Valerie know that there are two different versions of Habakkuk 2:4?"

"The findings of the cave four scrolls are still very fresh," her uncle explained. "It'll still take time for traditionalists to digest the voluminous information revealed by the Dead Sea Scrolls. But rest assured, the findings are conclusive and documented. It's only a matter of time."

"Thank you, Uncle Donny," Maria said with a hug. "I'm going to

---

60 See *The Jerome Conspiracy*

show Valerie that Paul's quote of Habakkuk 2:4 has been mistranslated because scholars didn't know they had a different version of Habakkuk 2:4 than Paul's. It all makes sense now."

Chapter 26

Although Valerie had already declared the debate over, Maria was determined — determined to get through to Valerie, determined to reconnect with Robert. Maria felt absolutely confident as she told Valerie over the phone, "The Bible doesn't say the righteous shall live by faith — that's a mistranslation."

"Where do you come up with that stuff?" Valerie said incredulously. "You think that any time a passage of the Bible doesn't agree with your pastor, it's due to a mistranslation?"

"No! It was my uncle who showed me the history of how this mistranslation took place. It's not a matter of theological debate. Rather, there are a set of documented historical events that led up to the mistranslation —."

"That's absolute nonsense and I'm certainly not interested at all in hearing any more. I've done my best to show you the truth, but you just stubbornly refuse to accept it. And now, you want me to believe that the Bible verse that ignited the Protestant Reformation is mistranslated! At this point, I have nothing more to say. Don't call again. Goodbye, Maria."

Despite knowing in her heart that she was completely correct on the historical matter, Maria felt that she had won the battle but lost the war. Her uncle's plan hadn't worked to hold onto her fiancé, and her trying to get closer to him by exploring the Bible had backfired. Robert was now lost to her forever.

¤ ¤ ¤

Patricia got up and walked into the kitchen to grab a diet soda. On her way to the refrigerator, she saw the stack of mail that Jack had put on the table. After grabbing the soda can, Patricia took a seat and began poring through the pile, cringing with each unpaid bill. Her hand started trembling when she came to an envelope sent from her landlord. A bead of perspiration trickled down her face as she opened it. She broke down when she read:

FINAL NOTICE

You are hereby warned that you have three days to pay back all due rent. If the full and total amount is not received by this time, eviction proceedings will begin the following morning. You will have 90 days from this notice to vacate the premises. If you have not vacated the premises by the 90th day, you will be escorted off the premises by the police.

Patricia looked toward the sky. "Why God? Why?"

Chapter 27

Three Months Later —

Patricia knocked on the apartment manager's door.

"What do you want?" the manager mumbled upon seeing her face.

"I know that you've done everything according to the law by sending me the final notice three months ago, and tomorrow, my time's up. Today's the last day before the police come to evict me and my son from our home."

"I'm sorry. I can't help you. You need to be out before five o'clock tomorrow," she said as she started closing the door.

Patricia put her foot in the door. "I've come here to make a deal with you."

"I'm listening."

"If I get a job by five o'clock tomorrow, and you let me stay in the apartment, I'll pay you an additional $100 a month that you can keep in your pocket, money that doesn't have to go to the owners of the apartment complex."

The apartment manager seemed to be considering the offer. "I don't know. I don't want to risk my job. But if you can prove to me that you have a job by five o'clock, I'll suspend the eviction. But you've got to start paying back the arrears, too. And if you're late on one more payment, I won't hesitate to reinstate the eviction immediately. Got that?"

¤ ¤ ¤

Robert could barely contain his excitement about leaving for the missionary trip with Valerie the following evening. All he had to do was make it through a lecture on commerce in the first century Roman Empire, sit an exam the next morning, then he was off on a great adventure with a fascinating, highly intelligent girl who had become the focus of his personal life.

The lecturer began. "Today, we're discussing the etymology of the Greek word *charagma* — we're going to explore how this word changed over time. It's always important for you to know how each word was used during the time period of the documents you are translating. And the Koine papyri, discovered in Egypt in the early 1900s, surprised scholars when it revealed a previously unknown usage of the Greek word *charagma* — a usage extremely popular in the first century Roman Empire."

Robert's ears perked up. He remembered that was one of the words in the passage from Valerie that had been bothering him for months:

> The Beast made it so that no one is able to buy or to sell, except the one who has **the mark [Greek: charagma]**: either the name of the Beast or the number of his name. And here is the sacred knowledge: Let anyone who is not mentally challenged calculate the number of the Beast, for the number is that of a man; and his number is six hundred and sixty-six.

The lecturer continued. "In ancient Greece, the word *charagma* originally referred to 'marks' and 'imprints'. However, over a span of hundreds of years, the word became most often associated with the imperial imprints on coins and contracts[61]. The Koine papyri showed that, by the first century, the word was commonly used as a technical business term referring to the imperial reference on the coins and contracts used in commerce. Prior to the discovery of the Koine papyri, scholars were not aware of this popular first century usage."

Robert carefully considered what he was hearing. The passage Valerie showed him was about buying and selling — commerce. And the first century Jewish readers of Revelation understood the meaning of the term *charagma* as it was used in commerce — a meaning they were intimately familiar with.

Robert grabbed a piece of paper and began to translate the

---

61 *Light from the Ancient East,* By Adolph Deissmann, Lionel Richard Mortimer Strachan, p. 341

Also: *A Greek English Lexicon,* by Liddell and Scott, entry for *charagma.*

Also: "Charagma was a technical term for the imperial stamp on commercial documents and the royal impression on Romans coins." *Revelation of Jesus Christ: Commentary on the Book of Revelation,* By Ranko Stefanović, p. 414

passage based on its first century meaning:

> The Beast made it so that no one is able to buy or to sell, except the one who has **the imperial imprint on the coins and contracts**: either the name of the Beast or the number of his name. And here is the sacred knowledge: Let anyone who is not mentally challenged calculate the number of the Beast, for the number is that of a man; and his number is six hundred and sixty-six.

The lecturer continued. "Let's consider the coins. One thing you'll note as you examine coins from the Roman Empire is that all the principal coins have an epigraph (a legend) on the front side of the coins. These epigraphs often contain the name of the Roman Emperor. Quite interestingly, we find written documentation about the use of the reigning emperor's name on the principle coins from the Christian Bible."

The lecturer provided the class with the following handout:

> "Tell us then, what do You think? Is it lawful to give a poll-tax to Caesar, or not?"
>
> But Jesus perceived their malice, and said, "Why are you testing Me, you hypocrites? **Show Me the coin used for the poll-tax.**"
>
> And **they brought Him a denarius**. And He said to them, "**Whose likeness and inscription is this?**"
>
> They said to Him, "**Caesar's.**"
>
> Then He said to them, "Then render to Caesar the things that are Caesar's; and to God the things that are God's."
>
> Matthew 22:17-21 NASB

The lecturer explained. "This Biblical passage is particularly interesting because the denarius 'was the most common coin produced for circulation.'[62] And this most common coin, as the Bible so correctly records, contained the image and the name of the reigning Emperor. And archaeology has confirmed the information in the Bible. Consider

62 *Coins, medals, and seals, ancient and modern: Illustrated and described*, by William Cowper Prime, p. 266.

See also *Classical antiquities*, by Johann Joachim Eschenburg, p. 267

this denarius minted during Nero's reign."

The lecturer handed out the following to her class:

When Robert saw the denarius, he all but jumped out of his seat. "The principle coins bore Nero's name on them during his reign?" he called out without even raising his hand.

"Oh yes," the teacher replied.

"So then, it would have been impossible to buy or sell without using coins with the imprint of Nero's name?" he asked rhetorically.

"Of course," his teacher affirmed. "You couldn't avoid the denarius and other principle coins."

Robert gulped as he realized Nero's name was imprinted on the front side of the coins during his reign. He re-examined the passage in light of this new information, underlining the part he now understood.

> The Beast made it so that no one is able to buy or to sell, except the one who has the coins and contracts bearing either the name of the Beast or the number of his name. And here is the sacred knowledge: Let anyone who is not mentally challenged calculate the number of the Beast, for the number is that of a man; and his number is six hundred and sixty-six.

Robert was beside himself. *Everything does point to Nero! he thought to himself. Nero must be the Beast! And since Nero's name was used on the coins, then that means the number of Nero's name must have been used on the contracts!* But Robert became deflated after he reread the part of the passage not underlined. The passage specifically said that the number of the Beast's name used in commerce was 666 — and Robert already knew that the number of Nero's Greek name was 1,332 and the number of Nero's Hebrew name was 616. "The number 666 is the most important clue to identifying the Beast, and Valerie already showed me that I'm wrong." Robert closed his Bible and returned his attention back to class.

The lecturer discussed many aspects of first century coinage — including the apparent discovery of a new mineral source and new methods of engraving images.[63] After a long, protracted discussion, the teacher then said, "And to round out our discussion of the *charagma* — the coins and contracts of first century commerce — I need to give you some highlights regarding the contracts used in the first century — because very recent archaeology has revealed another surprise to scholars."

Robert's ears perked up once again.

The teacher continued. "In recent times, a tremendous archaeological finding was unearthed in the Palestinian deserts — numerous Jewish contracts from the first few centuries were uncovered. And these contracts surprised scholars because they revealed something previously unknown to them — the official legal language of the Jewish community was Aramaic.[64] Up until the

---

63 *Nero: the end of a dynasty*, Griffin, p. 121
64 The Dead Sea Scrolls confirmed this as well. Three economic documents were found in the Dead Sea Scrolls from cave number four: 4Q345, 4Q346, and 4Q348. Two of these documents were legal bills of sale (4Q345 and 4Q346). Both of these were written entirely in Aramaic. The other document (4Q348) was a property deed primarily written in Hebrew, yet used Aramaic names and formulae to conform to court

destruction of Jerusalem in 70 AD, legally binding contracts were written in Aramaic. I now want you to turn your attention to this handout — a copy of a first century Aramaic contract."

The teacher then gave the students a photocopy of the Aramaic contract written in 56 AD — known in archaeological circles as: MUR 18.[65]

MUR 18
Aramaic Contract discovered in Murabbat

The year two of נ ר ו ק ס ר

At Siwaya, Absalom (son of Hannin from Siwaya) has declared in my presence that there is on account with me — me Zechariah (son of Yohannan, son of {illegible}) living at Cheaslon, the sum of twenty zuzin. The sum I am to repay by {illegible}. But if I have not paid by time, I will reimburse you with interest of a fifth and will settle in entirety, even if this is the Year of Release. And if I do not do so, indemnity for you will be from my possessions, and whatever I acquire will be at your disposal.

Zechariah, son of Yohannan, for himself.
Joseph, son of {illegible}, wrote this, witness.
Jonathan, son of John, witness.
Joseph, son of Judan, Judan, witness.

Robert couldn't believe what he was seeing: symbols that represented Nero's Aramaic name and the number of Nero's Aramaic name written at the top.

He asked another question. "Did every contract during Nero's reign have the symbols representing the *Aramaic* number of his name?"

"In the Jewish communities, yes," the lecturer replied. "The common convention of contracts was to include the identity of the reigning Emperor and the year of his reign. And since the official legal

---

standards. (For a discussion on the Aramaic parts of 4Q348, see *Judah and Judeans in the Fourth Century B.C.E.* by Oded Lipschitz, Gary N. Knoppers, Rainer Albertz, p. 115.)

65   *A Manual of Palestinian Aramaic Texts*, By Joseph A. Fitzmyer, Daniel J. Harrington, p. 136

language of the Jews was Aramaic, they used the name and number of the reigning Emperor using *Aramaic* symbols, of course."

Robert wrote out Nero's name in Aramaic and summed the symbols together.

נ	= 50
ר	= 200
ו	= 6
נ	= 50
ק	= 100
ס	= 60
ר	= 200
	= 666

Robert's hand was shaking as he looked at the number of Nero's name in Aramaic. For the sum was … 666. Robert couldn't believe that he was staring at a first century business contract with the number 666 written on it. Moreover, he couldn't believe that every single Jewish business contract bore the number 666. Of course only an imbecile wouldn't have understood the significance of this number during the time that John wrote about it.

Robert realized that every time Jews got a marriage certificate, they saw the Aramaic number of Nero's name: 666. And every time they got a divorce, they saw 666. Every time they bought a slave, they saw 666. And every time they sold a slave, they saw 666. Every time they adopted a child, they saw 666. Every time they incurred a debt, they saw 666. And every time they paid a debt, they saw 666. Every time they contracted to buy seeds in their agrarian society, they saw 666. And every time they contractually sold produce, they saw 666. Every time they issued a contract for the shipment of their goods, they saw 666. Every time they bought property, they saw 666. And every time they sold property, they saw 666.

Robert understood to his core how the Aramaic number of Nero's name — 666 — flooded their daily lives. *Truly only an imbecile would not have recognized the tyrant being referred to by 666 — the number of the Beast's name used in buying and selling,* Robert thought to himself.

Robert exited the class, fully aware that he knew the identity of the Beast of Revelation.

¤ ¤ ¤

Robert was in his room packing for the trip, when Valerie slipped silently through the door.

"What's that?" she asked, pointing to his desk.

"Oh, hi!" he said.

Valerie was picking up the birthday card from Maria. "Why have you still got this?" she asked.

Robert felt his cheeks redden. He could see the consternation on her face. "I don't know. I just do."

"You know, I never gave you the details of the last conversation I had with Maria. Would you believe she told me that her uncle said Martin Luther's great epiphany on Romans 1:17 — the epiphany that ignited the Protestant Reformation — was based on a mistranslation! Have you ever heard anything more ridiculous?"

Robert stood frozen for a moment. "Dr. Richmond told Maria *what*?"

"He convinced her that the verse which launched the Protestant Reformation was mistranslated. Crazy, huh?"

Robert looked Valerie squarely in the eyes. "Dr. Richmond may be many things, but careless with his words, never. And do you remember when I told you all those verses regarding the Beast of Revelation were mistranslated in your Bible?"

"Yes, but I also remember that the number 666 didn't add up. You were wrong."

"Well, today I discovered that 666 does add up and my findings were right all along." Robert explained how Aramaic contracts were the legal medium of exchange for the Jews prior to the fall of Jerusalem in 70 AD, and that during Nero's reign, every one of those contracts bore the Aramaic number of Nero's name — the number 666.

Valerie was ashen she listened.

Robert continued. "And when you told me that Dr. Richmond said that 'salvation by faith' is based on a mistranslation, it dawned on me — I haven't spent any time looking into the Greek Biblical texts on this matter. I've been so obsessed with the texts regarding the Beast of Revelation that I haven't really explored much else. But now that I realize the texts related to the Beast of Revelation are sorely mistranslated — many saying the very opposite of the Greek — it makes me wonder if it's possible that there are mistranslations on other topics too — including the topic of salvation itself."

"Wait a minute!" Valerie barked.

"No," Robert said sternly.   "I stopped looking for the mistranslations when you convinced me that 666 didn't add up. I know you weren't wrong intentionally — but you were wrong, nonetheless. And now that I'm questioning the translation of the Bible as a whole, I will not let you talk me out of finding the truth — wherever it may lead."

"But our missionary trip is tomorrow night!"

"Then that means I have only twenty-four hours to make up my mind. I'm going to see someone right now to help me get this sorted out once and for all. And you're going with me."

Chapter 28

Dr. Richmond invited Valerie and Robert into his office. "You said it was a matter of urgency."

Robert explained the situation.

"I have some materials here from my historical Jesus seminar that could prove useful," Dr. Richmond responded. "In this class, we examine the teachings of Jesus from a socio-historical perspective — independent of religious bias."

"But what's the difference?" Robert asked.

"The actual Jesus of history and the Jesus of modern religious institutions are very different. In fact, modern churches now have their version of Jesus promoting the very ideas that the historical Jesus dedicated his life to abolish."

"That's one of the most ridiculous things I've ever heard," Valerie huffed.

Dr. Richmond pulled a folder from his filing cabinet. "Let me give you some examples of the differences between the historical Jesus and the Jesus of modern Christianity. Some of the more interesting differences come from my lecture on Jesus' famous Sermon on the Mount."

Dr. Richmond handed Valerie and Robert a paper from the folder with the following:

> A good tree bringeth forth good fruit; but **a corrupt** tree bringeth forth **evil** fruit.... Every tree that bringeth not forth good fruit is hewn down, and cast into the fire.[66]

Then he explained. "This passage is rather amusing when you think about it. After all, how does one *corrupt* a tree? And how can fruit be *evil*? But what if I were to tell you that the word translated as 'corrupt' is the Koine Greek word *sapron*?"

Robert lit up. "Now that makes perfect sense."

---

66 Matthew 7:17, 19 KJV

Valerie looked puzzled.

Robert turned and explained to her. "The Koine word *sapron* described things that are *useless*.[67] Jesus was talking about useless trees, not corrupt ones."

Dr. Richmond nodded. "And Robert, what if I were to tell you that the word translated as 'evil' is the Koine word *poneros*?"

Robert grinned. "Oh, now that also makes sense."

"What does that Greek word mean?" Valerie asked.

Robert explained. "Do you remember the tons of Koine papyri discovered in the sands of Egypt that I told you about? Well, in the papyri, the Koine word *poneros* was used to describe something, or someone, that was *worthless*. For example, one papyrus author used the word *poneros* to describe his worthless assistant.[68] The assistant was neither evil nor immoral, but he was worthless."

Dr. Richmond explained the historical significance of the correct translation. "The Jewish nation was an agrarian society. Every year, the *useless* trees that bore *worthless* fruit were cut down and thrown into the fire. Only the trees that bore beautiful fruit (fruit that was edible and salable) were spared. Jesus used something the people were intimately familiar with to make his point. The historical Jesus actually taught:

> Every useful tree bears beautiful fruits. But the **useless** trees bear **worthless** fruit…. Every tree that does not bear beautiful fruit is cut down and thrown into the fire."

Dr. Richmond handed Valerie and Robert the following:

Who is Cut Down and Thrown into the Fire?

Historical Jesus: Those who are useless (those who do nothing to help others).

Religious Jesus: Those who are corrupt.

Then Dr. Richmond continued. "Now let me show you another example from Jesus' Sermon on the Mount."

---

67 *A Greek-English Lexicon of the New Testament and other Early Christian Literature, Third Edition,* p. 913.
68 Papyrus: PFouad 25 verso 1, 2

Dr. Richmond continued down the page of the King James Bible and showed Robert and Valerie the following:

> And then will I profess unto them, I never knew you: depart from me, ye that work **iniquity**.[69]

Then he explained. "According to the King James Bible, Jesus is going to cast away those who work 'iniquity'. This is the religious Jesus. But what if I were to tell you, Robert, that the word translated as 'iniquity' is the Koine word *anomian*?"

Robert had a puzzled look on his face. "That word means 'those who break the Law'.[70] So what Law was Jesus talking about?"

Dr. Richmond's grin spread from ear to ear. "Why don't you read Matthew 7:12, 23 from your Koine Greek Bible and translate it aloud for Valerie."

Robert read:

> Then, in everything, whatever you want people to do to you, do also to them **for this is the Law** ... And then I will declare to them, 'I never knew you. Get away from me **you who break the Law**.'

"Wow! What a difference!" Robert exclaimed. "The historical Jesus taught that those who don't treat others the way they want to be treated will be rejected on Judgment Day."

Valerie was speechless.

Dr. Richmond handed Robert and Valerie the following:

Who is Rejected on Judgment Day?

> *Historical Jesus:* Those who don't treat others the same way they want to be treated.
>
> *Religious Jesus:* Those who work iniqutiy.

Then Dr. Richmond turned to the beginning portion of Jesus' Sermon on the Mount. And he showed Robert and Valerie the following:

---

69 Mathew 7:23 KJV
70 *A Greek-English Lexicon of the New Testament and other Early Christian Literature, Third Edition,* p. 85

> For I say unto you, That except **your righteousness** shall exceed the righteousness of the scribes and Pharisees, ye shall in no case enter into the kingdom of heaven.[71]

Dr. Richmond turned in Robert's direction. "And what if I were to tell you that the word translated as 'righteousness' is the Koine word *dikaiosune*?"

"I'm not surprised!" Robert declared.

"Why?" Valerie asked. "What does that word mean?"

"*Dikaiosune* meant justice, equity, fairness,"[72] Robert replied. "Jesus was saying that unless his audience treated others more equitably than the scribes and the Pharisees, they would not enter the Kingdom of Heaven."

Robert opened his Koine Greek Bible to Matthew 5:20 and translated it aloud for Valerie.

> For I am telling you, unless **you treat people more equitably** than the Scribes and the Pharisees, you cannot enter the Kingdom of Heaven.

Then Dr. Richmond handed them the following:

Who Cannot Enter the Kingdom of Heaven?

Historical Jesus: Those who treat others inequitably.
Religious Jesus: Those who are morally unrighteous.

Dr. Richmond explained. "Jesus' Sermon on the Mount has been thoroughly rewritten by modern religious institutions. The historical Jesus taught that those who treat others inequitably cannot enter the Kingdom of Heaven. But the Jesus of religion says that the morally unrighteous cannot enter. The historical Jesus taught that those who don't treat others the way they want to be treated will be rejected on Judgment Day. But the religious Jesus says that the workers of iniquity will be rejected. The historical Jesus taught that the worthless — those who don't help others — will be cut down and thrown into the fire. But the Jesus of modern religion says that those who are corrupt will be cut

---

71 Matthew 5:20 KJV

72 *A Greek-English Lexicon of the New Testament and other Early Christian Literature, Third Edition,* p. 247

down and thrown into the fire."

Dr. Richmond handed Robert and Valerie the following:

Jesus' Sermon on the Mount
Actual Historical Jesus

Who's cut down and thrown into the fire?
    Those who are useless. (Those who do nothing to help others.)

Who's rejected on Judgment Day?
    Those who don't treat others the same way they want to be treated.

Who cannot enter the Kingdom of Heaven?
    Those who treat others inequitably.

Then Dr. Richmond turned to Valerie and asked, "What did the actual historical Jesus teach about salvation in his Sermon on the Mount?"

Valerie stared at the handout in silence.

"I'll give you all the time you need," Dr. Richmond assured her.

After a couple minutes, a tear descended down Valerie's cheek. "If this is what Jesus actually taught, and I trust Robert that it is, then he taught that salvation depends entirely on the equitable treatment of others. For only the inequitable are cut down and thrown into the fire — rejected on Judgment Day — unable to enter the Kingdom of Heaven."

Dr. Richmond then gave Robert and Valerie another handout:

Jesus' Sermon on the Mount
Rewritten Religious Jesus

Who's cut down and thrown into the fire?
    Those who are corrupt.

Who's rejected on Judgment Day?
    Those who work iniquity.

Who cannot enter the Kingdom of Heaven?
    Those who are morally unrighteous.

Then Dr. Richmond turned to Valerie and asked, "According to the King James Version of Jesus' Sermon on the Mount, what does the rewritten religious Jesus teach about salvation?"

Valerie became unglued. "Modern Bibles make it seem like Jesus' Sermon on the Mount was all about moral shortcomings, moral shortcomings that could be remedied through righteousness by faith. Modern Bibles have rewritten Jesus' teaching that treating others equitably is the key to entering the Kingdom of God. And now that I can see that the Bibles we use in our church have rewritten Jesus' teaching, I'm beginning to think they aren't really 'Bibles' at all."

Chapter 29

Valerie was trembling as she waited for her father to come to the phone. She almost fell apart as soon as she heard his voice, then did her best to explain. "My life's dream has been to save souls. But I just learned that the way we tell people to save their souls is very different than the message that Jesus taught. I just learned that Jesus taught that loving our neighbors as ourselves is the only commandment — the only deciding factor — just like Maria's pastor always said."

There was silence on the other end of the line. Then, finally, her father spoke. "Honey, I don't know how that liberal professor blinded you from the simple words that Jesus taught. Don't you remember what Jesus said is *the first and greatest commandment*?"

"Yes," Valerie managed. "Jesus taught that loving God with our whole heart, body, soul, and mind *is the first and greatest commandment*."

"That's right," her father affirmed. "And don't you remember Jesus said that loving your neighbor is only *the second* greatest commandment? So anyone who believes in the Bible cannot possibly say that loving your neighbor is the only commandment. In fact, Jesus specifically said it's not even the most important commandment. I don't know where Maria's pastor gets his theology from. But it's certainly not from the Bible."

Valerie's mind raced as she tried to make sense of what he was saying. Then it dawned on her. "You're right. Jesus did teach that loving your neighbor is only the second greatest commandment. I don't know how I could have forgotten that. Jesus couldn't have said anything to make it clearer that it's not the only commandment —nor even the most important one. Thank you, Dad."

¤ ¤ ¤

The moment Valerie finished her conversation with her father, she dialed Robert and explained that Jesus taught that loving your neighbor is only the second most important commandment.

"I'll be sure to ask Maria's pastor about that when I meet with him tomorrow," said Robert.

"What do you mean?"

"I've made an appointment to speak with Maria's pastor tomorrow at two o'clock. I want to find out everything I can about the Bible from him."

"But, Robert," Valerie said, "I just showed you Jesus said that pastor is wrong. Nothing could be simpler than the words that Jesus said: 'love of neighbor is the *second* commandment.' It's not the only, nor even the most important commandment."

Robert remained unfazed. "Fine. I'll just ask the pastor tomorrow if Jesus really said that."

Valerie was fuming. "Robert, I'm already telling you that's what Jesus said!"

Robert remained silent.

After a couple minutes of silence, Valerie asked, "Do you mind if my dad and I go to your meeting with Maria's pastor? I don't want this guy deceiving you — especially when the foundation of his theology contradicts a very straightforward statement from Jesus."

"I always believe that the fastest way to get to the truth is to hear all sides of a discussion at the same time," Robert replied. "See you there."

¤ ¤ ¤

Early the next morning, Patricia set out, determined to find a job. She knew that she only had until five o'clock before the police would come to evict her and her son. As she walked to the bus stop, she prayed the most fervent prayer of her life. "God, I trust you to help me take care of my boy. I leave his health and well-being in your perfect hands. Amen."

The morning proved tougher than Patricia had imagined. It seemed to her that every door was closing faster and harder than ever before. When she looked at her watch and saw that it was already 1:30PM, she said under her breath, "Are you testing my faith? Do you want to see if I can still believe up until the final minute? ... I still believe."

Chapter 30

"I see that we have a full house today," Pastor Tompkins said. "Everyone's welcome to take a seat."

After everyone was seated, Pastor Tompkins calmly turned to Robert. "Robert, what did the Koine Greek word *peirazon* mean when used in relation to first century Jewish lawyers?"

"To attempt to entrap through a process of inquiry[73]," Robert instantly answered.

Pastor Tompkins nodded. "I see that you brought a Greek Bible with you. Now that the others are also familiar with the Greek word *peirazon*, can you please translate Matthew 22:34-36?"

Robert translated the passage into English aloud:

> When the Pharisees heard Jesus had silenced the Sadducees, they gathered together in the same place.
>
> One of them, a lawyer, made an inquiry — **attempting to entrap him through his inquiry**. "Teacher, which is the great commandment of Law?"

Pastor Tompkins smiled then explained. "According to Matthew, the Lawyer set a trap for Jesus when he asked the question, 'What is the greatest commandment?' So here is the heart of the matter: what trap did the Pharisee set with his question? Why did the lawyer believe the answer to the question would instantly discredit Jesus? What teachings did the lawyer expect to destroy with the answer to that question? For it would be impossible to understand the wisdom of Jesus' response without first understanding the nature of the trap he so elegantly avoided."

No one knew the answer. After a few moments, Robert asked, "So what was the trap?"

Pastor Tompkins explained. "Jesus had been teaching that 'treating others the same way you want to be treated' — *treating others*

---

73   *A Greek lexicon of the New Testament and Other Early Christian Literature — Third Edition*, p. 793.

equitably — 'is the entire Law'.[74] Jesus also had been teaching that those who feed the hungry, clothe the naked, and shelter the homeless[75] — *those who treat others equitably* — are the ones who will inherit the kingdom. In the lawyer's mind, Jesus had left out man's obligation to God.

"So the Pharisaic lawyer set a trap for Jesus. The lawyer *wanted* Jesus to say, 'Love of God is the greatest commandment' — this was the trap! For once Jesus admitted this, the lawyer was ready to say, 'See, Jesus — you are wrong when you say that treating others equitably is the entire Law — the only commandment. And you are wrong when you say treating others equitably is the one deciding factor on Judgment Day. For you just admitted that there is another commandment — one that is even much more important than that. Ha! I got you!'"

Pastor Tompkins turned to Robert. "Now, please translate Matthew 22:34-39, staying true to the Greek while also making sure your translation shows that Jesus was getting out of the trap."

Robert translated the passage into English aloud:

When the Pharisees heard Jesus had silenced the Sadducees, they gathered together in the same place.

One of them, a lawyer, made an inquiry — attempting to entrap him through his inquiry. "Teacher, which is the great commandment of the Law?"

Jesus said to him, "'You shall love the Lord your God with all your heart, and with all your soul, and with all your mind.' This is the first and greatest commandment. Yet the second is its **equivalent**, 'you shall love your neighbor as yourself.'"

Pastor Tompkins explained. "Jesus escaped the trap in a brilliant way. First, he told the lawyer what the lawyer was expecting: love of God is the greatest commandment. And then he immediately injected a surprise: and loving your neighbor is its equivalent — it's the same thing. When you love your neighbor as yourself, you are loving God with an undivided heart. And this is why treating others

74 Matthew 7:12
75 "Then the King will say to those on his right, 'You who are blessed of my father, **come inherit the kingdom which was made for you since the beginning of the world because** I was hungry and you gave me something to eat; I was thirsty and you gave me something to drink; I was a stranger and you invited me in; [I was] naked and you clothed me; I was sick and you visited me; I was in prison and you came to me.'" (Matthew 25:34-36) Note: Jesus taught that those who are altruistic will inherit the kingdom **because** of their equitable deeds.

equitably is the entire Law — the only commandment. And this is why those who treat others equitably will inherit the Kingdom of God. This is why *there is only one commandment, only one deciding factor — love one another.*"

Valerie's father opened his Bible, the New International Version of the Bible, to the passage. After reading it, he looked up at Pastor Tompkins and said, "My Bible translates that passage differently. According to my Bible, Jesus says, 'the second commandment *is like* the first.'"

"Think about what that translation does!" Pastor Tompkins exclaimed. "The lawyer wanted to force Jesus to backtrack on his teaching that treating others as you want them to treat you is the Law. The lawyer wanted Jesus to backtrack on his teaching that only those who treat others equitably inherit the kingdom. And now *the translation in your Bible is doing the job for him*! That translation has Jesus falling prey to the trap that Matthew said Jesus avoided. That translation has not only missed the point, it even promotes the very idea that Jesus was refuting — the idea of God first, neighbor second. Jesus was against that idea and the Pharisees hated him for it."

"This is absurd!" cried Valerie's father. Turning to Valerie, he said, "Let's get out of here. These liberals are more screwed up than I could have ever imagined."

"Twenty-four hours ago, I would have agreed with you, Dad," Valerie replied. "But I've seen for myself that the original Christian Bible — the Koine Greek Bible — shows Jesus taught very different things than our 'Bibles' say. You taught me to place my faith in the teachings of Christ no matter what — no matter what my church may say and no matter what my parents say. And I'm staying, Dad. I have a very big question to ask Pastor Tompkins."

Her father was stunned. "What question?"

"I want to ask the pastor what I must do to be saved," she told him.

"Are you crazy?"

"No, Dad," she replied. "I finally understand the Bible like never before."

"We'll talk about this later," her father stammered. "I've already had all I can stand."

Valerie's father stormed out of the church.

Robert turned to Maria. "Is there any way you could ever possibly find it in your heart to forgive me?"

"I don't need to forgive you for trying to do the right thing," Maria replied. "It's one of the reasons why I fell in love with you and why I stayed in love with you all this time. You're an amazing guy, Robert, and I love you."

Robert and Maria embraced.

Maria looked at her watch. "I'm sorry. I have to go. Tonight is one of my shifts at the food shelter."

"Can I see you after you're done there?" Robert asked.

"Nothing would make me happier," Maria replied. Turning toward the group, she said, "Goodbye, everyone." And she left.

¤ ¤ ¤

Patricia glanced at her watch: it was already past 3:00 PM.

"God, *please* help me. I'm going to have to head home soon, and if I return without a job, my son is going to be homeless. I've been doing my part, looking for days. *Please*, I'm begging you."

Chapter 31

"I'm sorry to bother you so late in your office," Robert told Dr. Richmond.

"Seeing my future 'nephew in law' can never be a bother," Dr. Richmond said, breaking into a wide smile.

"Maria called you?"

"The moment she left the church," he replied. "I couldn't be happier to know that the two of you are back together." Then he paused for a moment. "I never got a chance to tell you how truly sorry I am for the loss of your mother. I'm sure she would be absolutely delighted to see what a fine scholar and devout Christian you are."

"Thank you."

"So to what do I owe this visit?"

Robert explained. "Ever since I learned that the entire topic of the Beast of Revelation has been rewritten in modern Bibles, I've been very upset. And now that I've learned that the topic of salvation has been rewritten as well, I just have to know how all of this happened. How is it possible that wholesale changes to the Bible seem to have been made from beginning to end?"

"Fortunately, there is a very straightforward answer to your question. By comparing the four most influential versions of the Bible to each other, you can see for yourself how all of this happened."

"I don't understand," said Robert.

Dr. Richmond clarified. "The original Bible was written in Greek in the first century. From that time until the present, there have been four versions of the Bible that have shaped Western Christianity — and thereby, the world."

Dr. Richmond handed Robert the following:

The Bibles That Shaped the World

First century: The original *Koine Greek Bible*, which served as the official text of Christianity for the first four hundred years of the faith.

Fifth century: The *Latin Vulgate*, which served as the only Bible in Western Christianity for more than one thousand years.

Seventeenth century: The *King James Version*, which served as the standard Bible for the Western Protestant Christians for three hundred years.

Twentieth century: The *New International Version*, which is currently the single most popular Bible.

Then he explained. "We can learn a lot about the historical evolution of Christian doctrine by comparing the Bibles from different time periods to each other."

"That makes sense."

"In one of my religious history classes, we do a very thorough job of comparing these four texts against one another. But for now, let me share a couple interesting insights with you. Let's start by comparing Romans 6:13 as it's found in the *Latin Vulgate* to the way it's written in the *King James Version*. As an ancient language major, can you tell me where we get the English word 'inequity' from, the word that means treating other people less equally?"

"Of course," Robert immediately replied. "That word comes from the Latin word *iniquitas*. And the Latin word *iniquitas* meant: injustice, unfairness, inequality.[76]"

Dr. Richmond lifted a copy of the *Latin Vulgate* from his bookshelf and turned to Romans 6:13. Then he asked Robert to translate the beginning part.

Robert translated the beginning words aloud:

Neither yield your members as instruments of **inequity** unto sin…

Dr. Richmond nodded. "That's right. According to the *Latin Vulgate*, Romans 6:13 says to avoid the sin of inequity — the sin of treating others less equally than yourself." He paused for a moment

---

76 **iniquitās, ātis** *f* inequality; unfairness — *Oxford Latin Desk Dictionary*, Copyright 2005, p. 95

Also: **Iniquitās, tātis** f *unfairness, injustice, unreasonableness — Cassell's Latin Dictionary*, p.308

and then asked, "And Robert, what was the Latin word for the opposite
— the word for the just, fair, equitable treatment of others?"

"*Iustitia[77],*" Robert immediately replied.

Dr. Richmond grinned. "And with this in mind, now please
translate the entire verse."

Robert translated the entire verse aloud:

> Neither yield your members as instruments of **inequity** unto sin: but
> present yourselves to God as those who are alive from the dead; and your
> members as instruments of **justice, fairness, equity** unto God.

Dr. Richmond explained. "According to the Latin Vulgate,
Romans 6:13 tells its readers to abandon inequitable (unequal)
treatment of others and to become instruments of justice, fairness,
equity — they must feed the hungry, clothe the naked, shelter the
homeless, and so on."

"That sure matches what Jesus taught," Robert interjected.

Dr. Richmond took a copy of the seventeenth century *King
James Version* of the Bible and opened it to Romans 6:13. Then he
asked Robert to read the passage aloud.

Robert read:

> Neither yield ye your members as instruments of **unrighteousness** unto
> sin: but yield yourselves unto God, as those that are alive from the dead, and
> your members as instruments of **righteousness** unto God.

Then Dr. Richmond explained. "Do you see how the King
James Bible has completely changed the message? The Latin Vulgate
told the Romans to leave the sin of treating others inequitably, while
the King James Bible says that the Romans must leave the sin of moral
'unrighteousness'. And the Latin Vulgate said the remedy of sin is to
become an instrument of justice, fairness, equity, while the King James
Bible says the remedy is to become morally 'righteous'. The King James
Bible has rewritten the Christian responsibility towards his neighbors
as a demand for obedience to the moral rulebook of God."

---

77 **Iūstitia, ae** *f* justice, equity — *Oxford Latin Desk Dictionary*, Copyright 2005, p. 102

Also: **Iustitia —ae** f (iustus), *justice, fairness, equity* - *Cassell's Latin Dictionary*, p. 331

"Fascinating," was all Robert could say, as he compared the vast differences between the two passages.

Dr. Richmond paused a moment to allow Robert to digest the implications of what he had just read. Then he asked, "Now, Robert, what significant event happened in Christian history between the fifth century writing of the Latin Vulgate and the seventeenth century writing of the King James Version?"

"The Protestant Reformation," Robert immediately replied.

"That's right," Dr. Richmond affirmed. "And with the Protestant Reformation, charity as a requirement for salvation was tossed into the trash. And with this change in doctrine came accompanying changes to the Bible as well."

Robert compared the two versions one more time. "Plain as day."

Dr. Richmond nodded. "And do you remember what I showed you and Valerie from my class on Jesus' Sermon on the Mount?"

"Of course," Robert replied. "You showed me that Jesus' teachings about treating others equitably have all been rewritten as diatribes against moral unrighteous. And now I see Paul's words were changed in the exact same way."

Dr. Richmond observed the knowing look in Robert's eyes. "So you see, Robert, the Protestant Reformation replaced the Biblical doctrine of salvation by love and justice with the teaching of salvation by faith and moral righteousness. When the doctrines changed, the Bible was changed as well."

"And what about the Apocalypse and the Beast of Revelation?" Robert asked. "Why have these topics been rewritten?"

"You'll find the answer to your question by comparing the King James Version to the New International Version." Dr. Richmond opened the King James Bible to Matthew 24:28. Then he asked Robert to read it aloud.

Robert read:

For wherever the carcass is, there will **the eagles** be gathered together.

Then Dr. Richmond asked, "Those words were spoken by Jesus in the first century. Can you tell me what those words mean?"

"That's easy. Any student of Roman history would know

what that means," said Robert. "The Roman army always marched with numerous huge drawings of eagles that could be seen from great distances. People knew that wherever they saw those eagles gathered together, a lot of human carcasses were there too."

Dr. Richmond nodded, indicating that Robert had hit the nail on the head. Then he handed Robert a copy of the New International Version of the Bible and said, "Now read the same verse in this Bible."

Robert read:

> Wherever there is a carcass, there **the vultures** will be.

Robert got a confused look on his face. "The New International Version has changed the word 'eagles' to 'vultures'. How is that possible? They are two totally different animals, with two totally different Greek words. One of these versions is simply wrong." Robert hurriedly grabbed his Greek Bible and turned to the passage. Then he exclaimed, "The Greek says *aetos*, which means 'eagles'.[78] That word can never be translated as 'vultures' — so why did the New International Version invent its own meaning for the word?"

Dr. Richmond smiled. "The King James Version was written in the seventeenth century. Then later, in the nineteenth century, a major doctrinal change occurred in the Protestant faith — the doctrine of the Rapture was born. And in order for this doctrine to take root, certain passages in the Bible referring to first century events had to be rewritten as events that were to occur in the future — at the end of time. And that includes the events of Matthew chapter twenty-four.

"Jesus' words were a problem for the new doctrine. For as long as Jesus' words are translated correctly, it's clear that he was referring to the Roman eagles — and it's clear that the events he was describing occurred during the existence of the Roman Empire. So the New International Version conveniently changed the animal from 'eagles' to 'vultures' — allowing the passage to be interpreted as a still unfulfilled future event. With another change in doctrine came other accompanying changes to the Bible as well."

Robert was fuming. He opened the King James Version to the book of Revelation and then he opened the New International Version to the book of Revelation as well. Then he laid them side-by-side. "I

---

78 *A Greek English Lexicon*, Liddell and Scott, p. 29

knew it!" he exclaimed, as he compared the differences:

> *16th Century KJV* - And the Beast that was, and is not, even he is **the eighth,** and is **of the seven**, and goeth into perdition.

> *21st Century NIV* - The Beast who once was, and now is not, **is an eighth king**. He belongs to the seven and is going to his destruction.

"What did you find?" Dr. Richmond asked.

Robert explained. "The original Greek says that the Beast is the one of seven kings who is the eighth, meaning that the number of his name is the eighth triangular unit. The King James Version is correct. But the New International Version has changed the meaning of the passage entirely. It says that while the Beast belongs to the seven kings, he's still going to be a future eighth king. You're right. When the doctrine changed — when the Rapture theology was born — accompanying changes were made to the Bible to promote the new belief."

Dr. Richmond was all aglow. "You got it."

"So the Latin Vulgate is the only accurate translation?" Robert asked.

Dr. Richmond shook his head from side-to-side. "Even it had already deviated from the original Greek."

"How so?"

Dr. Richmond explained. "The original Bible was penned in Greek during the first century. It taught that Christ's return would usher in an age of punishment and special reward. The punishment was called 'the punishment of the age' and the special reward was called 'the life of the age'.[79] Second century documents showed that mainstream Christians in both the East and the West all believed in this age of special reward and punishment. And they believed that after this age was over, all souls would enjoy eternal friendship with God.[80]

"But in the fifth century, a new doctrine was foisted upon Christianity — the doctrine of eternal punishment and exclusive eternal reward. And with this change in doctrine came accompanying

---

79 See *The Jerome Conspiracy*
80 See *The Jerome Conspiracy*

changes to the Bible as well. The fifth century Latin Vulgate Bible was written with edits made to the passages on punishment and special reward.[81]"

Robert's eyes widened. "So at each stage of Christian history, doctrinal changes resulted in an increasing number of changes made to the Bible itself."

Dr. Richmond walked over to the blackboard, then said, "Give me a moment to draw this out for you so you can see for yourself how modern Bibles got to be the way they are now."

---

81 See *The Jerome Conspiracy*

How the Christian Bible Changed over Time

	1st Century Original Greek	5th Century Latin Vulgate	17th Century King James	20th Century NIV
Mt 25:46	The unjust suffer the punishment of the age.	The unjust suffer eternal punishment.	The unjust suffer eternal punishment.	The unjust suffer eternal punishment.
Mt 25:46	The just are rewarded with the life of the age.	The just are rewarded with eternal life.	The just are rewarded with eternal life.	The just are rewarded with eternal life.
Ro 6:13	The Romans were told to stop using the members of their bodies for the inequitable treatment of others.	The Romans were told to stop using the members of their bodies for the inequitable treatment of others.	The Romans were commanded not to use their bodies for moral unrighteousness.	The Romans were commanded not to use their bodies for moral unrighteousness.
Ro 6:13	The Romans were commanded to use the members of their bodies as instruments of justice, fairness, equity.	The Romans were commanded to use the members of their bodies as instruments of justice, fairness, equity.	The Romans were commanded to yield their bodies as instruments of moral righteousness.	The Romans were commanded to yield their bodies as instruments of moral righteousness.
Mt 24:28	At the end of the age, where the eagles are — so are the carcasses.	At the end of the age, where the eagles are — so are the carcasses.	At the end of the age, where the eagles are — so are the carcasses.	At the end of the age, where the vultures are — so are the carcasses.
Re 17:11	The Beast of Revelation is an eighth.	The Beast of Revelation is an eighth.	The Beast of Revelation is an eighth.	The Beast of Revelation is an eighth king.

After giving Robert a moment to digest the table, Dr. Richmond said, "Maybe it would be easier to visualize if I erase each place where a change was made."

How the teachings of the Bible Disappeared over Time

	1st Century Original Greek	5th Century Latin Vulgate	17th Century King James	20th Century NIV
Mt 25:46	The unjust suffer the punishment of the age.	-	-	-
Mt 25:46	The just are rewarded with the life of the age.	-	-	-
Ro 6:13	The Romans were told to stop using the members of their bodies for the inequitable treatment of others.	The Romans were told to stop using the members of their bodies for the inequitable treatment of others.	-	-
Ro 6:13	The Romans were commanded to use the members of their bodies as instruments of justice, fairness, equity.	The Romans were commanded to use the members of their bodies as instruments of justice, fairness, equity.	-	-
Mt 24:28	At the end of the age, where the eagles are — so are the carcasses.	At the end of the age, where the eagles are — so are the carcasses.	At the end of the age, where the eagles are — so are the carcasses.	-
Re 17:11	The Beast of Revelation is an eighth.	The Beast of Revelation is an eighth.	The Beast of Revelation is an eighth.	-

"Oh my God!" Robert exclaimed. "As time marched on, Bibles got further and further away from the original text. Almost none of the original teachings even remain. Modern versions aren't really 'Bibles' at all."

"That's right," Dr. Richmond said, while staring at the table. "Where the original Bible spoke of proportionate punishment and proportionate reward, the modern Bible now speaks of eternal punishment and eternal reward. Where the original Bible taught that those who contribute to the material needs of others in this life will receive a great reward in the next, the modern Bible now speaks of a salvation from the consequences of moral shortcomings through righteousness imputed by faith. Where the original Bible envisioned Christians transforming the earth, the modern Bible now speaks of a God who destroys the earth in a violent apocalypse. Almost all the teachings of the original Bible are completely hidden from modern congregants."

Chapter 32

Valerie repeated her question to Pastor Tompkins. "Pastor, please tell me, what does the original Bible say a person must do to be a Christian?"

"Let me tell you what Paul wrote about being saved. His theology on salvation revolved around the Greek word *pistis*. And it's impossible to understand what Paul wrote without first having a thorough understanding of this word."

"Isn't that the Greek word that meant 'faith'?"

"The Greek word *pistis* meant much more than that," the pastor replied. "It embodied three aspects all at the same time: faith, pledge, and faithfulness. The word embodied all the requirements for becoming a member of a covenant. Covenantal initiates needed to: *believe in* the covenantal Law, *pledge* to follow it, and remain *faithful* to it. And Paul, who believed Jesus had brought a new covenant, chose this word to describe salvation as becoming a member of a new covenant; a convert must: believe in the Law of Christ, pledge to follow it, and remain faithful to it."

"Makes sense," Valerie remarked.

"Paul's letter to the Romans was written to warn Christians that the only way to avoid God's wrath is to embrace all three aspects of the word; Christians must believe, pledge, and be faithful. In chapters one and two, Paul warns the Romans that if they do not move beyond belief and a mere pledge into faithfulness, then they would most assuredly suffer God's wrath. In Romans chapters three through six, Paul told them that the moment they believed in the gospel and pledged to follow it, all their prior sins were instantly covered by the atonement of Christ as a free gift. Then, in Romans chapters six through eight, Paul explained that only by remaining faithful from that day forward could their record remain clean. This was Paul's explanation of how to be saved and remain saved: you must believe in the Law of Christ, pledge to follow it and remain faithful to it. Make sense?"

"Yes."

The pastor's voice assumed a very serious tone. "So Valerie, do you believe the Law of Christ? — do you believe that *there is only one commandment, only one deciding factor — love one another?*"

Valerie thought through all that she had learned since meeting Maria. "Yes, I really do believe that now."

A smile came across the pastor's face. "And are you willing to repent? Are you willing to pledge to love your neighbor as yourself from this day forward for the rest of your life?"

A tear fell from Valerie's face. "Yes, for Jesus' sake, I do."

The pastor's smile widened. "Then according to Paul's theology, you are now saved — your entire slate has been wiped clean. But I must remind you that you have to be faithful if you want to keep your record clean."

"If I must be faithful to be saved from God's wrath, what exactly must I do?"

Pastor Tompkins reached for his Bible. "In the Biblical book of Luke, a group of people asked Jesus that very same question."

Jesus told the crowd, "Indeed the axe is already laid at the root of the trees; so every tree that does not bear useful fruit is cut down and thrown into the fire."

And the crowd questioned him, saying, "**Then what shall we do?**"

And he answered and said to them, "The man who has two coats is to share with him who has none; and he who has food is to do likewise." Luke 3:9-11

Valerie shook her head. "I can't tell you how many times I read that passage and just mentally skipped right over it. But now, for the first time, I can finally see that the crowd asked Jesus what they must do to avoid being thrown into the fire — *they asked Jesus how to be saved from the wrath of God.* And now I can see Jesus' answer had nothing to do with faith. Jesus' answer was based on the command to love our neighbors as ourselves, for if we love our neighbors as much as our own selves, we couldn't possibly hold onto anything extra."

The pastor nodded. "This is always the first passage I share with new converts, because it gives such practical instructions on how to be saved from the fire. I encourage all new converts to constantly make an inventory of all their extras — extra time, extra clothes, extra money, etcetera — and then share them freely — and secretly — with those in need."

Valerie looked up at the poster behind the pastor. "I really can see that when the crowd asked Jesus how to be saved, his answer was based on the assumption that *there is only one commandment, only one deciding factor — love one another.* And I vow, from this moment on, to freely and secretly share my extras with others who need them."

"Welcome to the family of Christ," Pastor Tompkins said.

Chapter 33

Patricia used her final dollar to get on the bus and head home. As she took her seat, she glanced at her watch. "Oh, God! It's almost five o'clock. I hope the police don't come while Jack is there all by himself."

Patricia exited the bus one block from the apartment complex. She saw Jack standing next to a police officer and two pieces of luggage.

She ran to her son. "I'm so sorry for all this," she said, while fighting back the tears.

"I packed as much as I could, Mom," said Jack Jr.

Patricia turned to the officer. "Can I go in and check to see if my son missed anything important?"

"The locks have already been changed," the officer replied. "That's no longer your property and I can't allow you to go in there."

Patricia picked up the two pieces of luggage and turned to her son. "Let's go."

"Where, Mom?"

"I don't know, honey. I don't have any money for the bus."

"You don't have any relatives you can stay with?" the officer asked.

"No," Patricia replied. "We have no place to go."

"I know where you and your son can get food and shelter for the night," the officer said, while taking one of the pieces of luggage from Patricia's hand. "I can drive you and your son there."

"Thank you."

¤ ¤ ¤

Maria was setting up the food line at the shelter. She was startled when she saw Robert come in.

Maria ran over and greeted Robert with a hug and kiss.

"Can you guys use some extra help?" Robert asked.

"Always!" Maria replied. "And I couldn't be happier to see you here."

"You'll be seeing me here much more often, honey," Robert told her. "I'd like us to work together as a team, helping those who need it."

"Aren't you forgetting something?" said Maria.

"What?" Robert asked.

Maria extended her left ring finger.

With a big goofy grin, Robert reached into his pocket, pulled out the engagement ring, and slipped it onto Maria's finger. "I love you."

"I love you, too, and I always will."

Robert and Maria held each other in their arms. Their embrace was interrupted when Maria saw Patricia enter the shelter. "Robert, look!" she said, while pointing over to Patricia. "It's the waitress from Sammy's."

¤ ¤ ¤

When Valerie got home, she unpacked the clothes she had prepared for her missionary trip. And she also unpacked the bundle of mail that she had set aside to go through on the plane. As she sorted the mail, she noticed there was an envelope from Maria.

What's this? she wondered.

When Valerie opened the envelope, she found a birthday card and a note. Valerie read the note with tears streaming down her face.

Dear Valerie,

My greatest hope for Robert has always been for his happiness. I know Robert was never at peace with our relationship because of his mother's strong influence. Robert always wished that she would be proud of all the choices he made. And now, thanks to his relationship with you, I can see he has finally found the peace he was always desperately searching for.

Finally seeing Robert at peace, I find myself grateful that you have come into his life.

Sincerely,
Maria Richmond

Chapter 34

Patricia tried to convey to Maria all the trauma that she and Jack had been going through. She also explained how the doctor was able to reduce the cost of the surgery to thirty thousand dollars, but that was an impossible amount.

"But I do want to thank you for trying to help us," Patricia told her. "You have no idea how much that means to me."

Maria placed her hand on top of Patricia's. "I wish there was more I could do to help."

Just then, Valerie walked into the shelter.

Maria excused herself and walked over to Valerie. "Did you miss your flight?" Maria asked.

"No. I decided not to go," Valerie replied. "If I went on the missionary trip, I'd be required to teach people a false salvation. And now, I want to dedicate my life to lifting burdens and teaching others to do the same."

"I'm proud to know you, Valerie," Maria said, as she placed her hand upon Valerie's shoulder.

"I feel the same," Valerie responded. "When I got home, I went through the mail I was saving up and found this wonderful letter you wrote to me. And I came here to thank you for your kindness. And I also came to apologize for any rudeness I might have shown during our theological debates."

"You have no need to apologize for anything," Maria said. "You really believed what you were told, and you were trying to do what you believed was best for my soul. I appreciated the effort, however misguided it might have been."

"Robert is a lucky guy to have you as a fiancée," Valerie said, before turning around to leave.

"And Robert is lucky to have you as a friend," Maria called out after her. "Please don't leave without saying 'hi' to him. He's in the kitchen, and I know he'd be hurt to hear you came by without talking to him."

Valerie turned back around, gave Maria a smile, and walked to the kitchen. When she opened the door, she found Robert getting ready to tackle a mountain of dirty dishes. "I'll wash, you dry," Valerie said as she approached him.

The sound of Valerie's voice startled Robert. "Aren't you going to miss your flight?"

"I'm not going on the missionary trip," she replied. "If I go, I'd have to teach my church's version of salvation, which isn't salvation at all."

Robert handed her a dishcloth.

A short while into the cleanup, Valerie said, "Isn't that the waitress from Sammy's I saw out there?"

"Yes," Robert affirmed. "I talked to her earlier."

Robert explained Patricia's plight, including her need of $30,000 to save her son's life.

"That's really sad," Valerie said, as a tear descended down her cheek.

The two remained silent for a while as they tackled more dirty dishes.

Then Robert paused and looked Valerie squarely in the eyes. "You know, I have to say how impressed I am with you. I know how much you've sacrificed to save money for your missionary trip: you've lived with your parents to save on rent; you packed all your own lunches to save money on food; you never bought a car. You've sacrificed years of doing nothing but working to set aside money for your missionary work."

"That's true," said Valerie. "And now that I've saved up more than $50,000, I don't know what I'm going to do with all that extra cash."

The moment Valerie said the word 'extra', her mind flashed back to her conversation with the pastor. She recalled her vow to share, in secret, all her extras. And then her mind immediately shifted to Patricia.

"Do you know the waitress' name?" she asked Robert.

"Yes," he replied. "It's Patricia. Patricia Jackson."

"Thanks, I gotta go," Valerie told Robert before abruptly leaving the kitchen.

¤ ¤ ¤

Valerie walked to a quiet corner of the shelter to remove her checkbook from her purse. She wrote a check for $40,000 made payable to Patricia Jackson.

Then she walked over to Patricia and explained that if she brought the check to her bank tomorrow, she would be able to withdraw the funds immediately. She also asked Patricia to keep the whole thing a secret between themselves. Then she hugged Patricia and left.

Chapter 35

On Sunday morning, Valerie walked into the foyer of Maria's church and was warmly greeted by many of the congregants. As she headed toward the sanctuary, Maria walked straight over to her and gave her a big hug.

"Thank you," Valerie said. "But what was that for?"

"Patricia told me what you did for her son," Maria said with misty eyes. "I keep thanking God for you, Valerie. And if the struggles that Robert and I went through had to happen for you to cross Patricia's path, then it was all worth it." Maria took Valerie by the hand. "Would you like to sit with Robert and me during the service?"

¤ ¤ ¤

At the end of the morning service, the pastor rose and gave a short sermon:

"The foundation of the Jewish Law was Moses' famous Ten Commandments. And, quite naturally, the most important commandment was the first one, the commandment against idolatry. In the Law of Moses, there simply was no greater sin than idolatry — the sin of putting anything else before God.

"But here is a great question: what happened to the greatest sin, the sin of idolatry, after Christ delivered his Law? After all, Christ taught that his entire Law is fulfilled by loving our neighbors as ourselves. And the original definition of idolatry doesn't directly violate the new Law of Christ.

"To find our answer, we need to remember why Jesus said that loving our neighbor fulfills the whole Law. Jesus said that treating others the way we want to be treated is the Law, because whatever we do to our neighbors, we are doing to God.[82] In other words, if we inflict harm on our neighbors, we are hurting God himself. If we show

---

82 Matthew 25:40

contempt to our neighbor, we are showing our disdain to God himself. And if we hoard things away from our neighbor, we are valuing things above God himself. In other words, if we are greedy — if we hoard things from our neighbor — then we are committing the worst possible sin, the sin of idolatry, because we are valuing things over God himself.

"Is this crazy talk? Did the earliest Christians really understand the Law of Christ in this way? Allow me to introduce you to the words of one of the earliest Christians from the first century. This first century Christian leader told his followers:

Consider your earthly bodies dead to **greed, which is idolatry**.

"According to this first century author, hoarding things away from your neighbor was idolatry under the new Law of Christ. This writer really believed that Christ's Law was based on the premise that whatever we do to our neighbor, we do to God himself.

"So who was this Christian author? ... It's none other than the Apostle Paul himself, the man who wrote the most books in the Bible.

"This week, I want you to take time each day to contemplate the significance of Paul's words: 'greed, which amounts to idolatry.' Meditate on them. The more you do so, the more clearly you'll see that Paul's theology is based on the premise that what we do to our neighbor, we are doing to God himself. In Paul's theology, there is no separation between loving your neighbor and loving God. The way to love God is through our neighbor; the way to serve God is by serving our neighbor. And if we withhold anything from our neighbor, we are withholding from God himself. Because of the new Law of Christ, greed is the new idolatry.

"I also want you to take time to think about what this means, in terms of all the other requirements in the Law of Moses. If the single most important Law, the Law against idolatry, has been redefined in terms of our neighbor, then all the other laws must be redefined in terms of our neighbor as well.

"When you realize that everything goes back to the way we treat our neighbors, you will awaken to the beautiful and profound Law of Christ. And I pray that, in doing so, you'll find that this realization transforms the way you live the rest of your life."

The pastor motioned for the congregation to stand. Then,

as was the custom every Sunday, they all recited in unison, "There is *only one commandment, only one deciding factor — love one another.* Amen."

¤ ¤ ¤

Robert and Maria drove from the church parking lot and headed in the direction of Sammy's for lunch.

"What a great sermon in church today, didn't you think?" Maria remarked.

"It sure was," Robert agreed. "And you know, it's sad that my mom never got to meet Pastor Tompkins. I'm sure she would have recognized his love for Christ and his love for the Bible. And he probably could have gotten through to her. How different everything could have been. It's been bothering me every day that Mom's last words to me were, 'I'm so disappointed in you, Robert.' I would give anything to be able to turn back time and redo everything that happened that day."

Maria placed her hand on Robert's thigh. "Honey, don't beat yourself up like that."

"I can't help it," Robert replied. "Sometimes, I wonder if it was her anger at me that pushed her over the edge — that caused her to die. I just can't get over the thought that I caused my mom's last moments to be so miserable. I know I'm going to regret it for the rest of my life."

Chapter 38

Robert and Maria spent the next months making wedding plans. As Maria's mother had passed on, they decided to make all the arrangements together, as a couple.

At the bakery, while they were selecting wedding cakes, Robert got a phone call.

"Thank you for the notice," he said into the phone. "I'll take care of it."

"Who was that?" Maria asked.

"It was the realtor on mom's house; it's been sold. I'm going to have to go back and prepare the house for the closing."

"You mean, *we* will go back," Maria said, putting her arms around him.

Robert hugged her back. "Honey, there're so many things that will have to be sorted out at the house before the closing. And we also need to finish the wedding plans. How about if I fly back and sort through Mom's personal stuff while you take care of the wedding arrangements here?"

"I hate the thought of you going back there by yourself. I know you've been avoiding it ever since your mom passed."

"The time has come for me to face all the memories, Babe. I'll be fine."

¤ ¤ ¤

Robert sat in the car outside his mother's house for almost an hour before he finally mustered up the courage and went inside.

"Might as well get the most difficult room out of the way first," he mumbled to himself.

He walked upstairs and stood at the entranceway to his mother's bedroom — the room in which he had found her lifeless body. Robert took a deep breath and went inside. After emptying the dresser, he began working on the closet. Not surprisingly, he found that it was filled with journals his mother had filled over the years. He packed them.

Then, after finishing the closet, Robert went to the nightstand. On top was his mother's final journal — the journal she had been writing in the night she was upset with Robert, the night she had passed on.

Robert's hands were trembling as he lifted the journal from the nightstand. The realization that it contained his mother's last words both haunted him and filled him with curiosity at the same time. Curiosity won the day. Robert opened the journal and found the final entries his mother wrote:

> *Sunday, 6:30 PM*
> *I only have a little time left and I'm starting to believe that I'm not going to be reunited with Robert in heaven. I can't take it, God. How can I say goodbye to him and never see him again? This is so unfair. I've been pleading for you to save him every day for years. God, please, tell me what to do. That Maria has too much influence over him.*

> *Sunday, 7:00 PM*
> *Thank you, God! I don't know why I never realized before that the only way to get through to Robert is to go through Maria. I need to show her that her church doesn't follow the Bible. But how can I do that? I really don't have a lot of time.*

> *Sunday, 7:15 PM*
> *But of course! Maria's a smart girl. I just need to overwhelm her with the evidence and I'm sure she'll come around.*
> *The New Testament is quite short. God, I commit this plan into your hands. I will read the New Testament from beginning to end and record every place where you tell us how to be saved. I trust you to open Maria's eyes when she sees the overwhelming weight of scripture.*
> *Let me start with Matthew, the first book of the New Testament.*
> *Got it. This is the first place that mentions the method*

of salvation.

> *But when John saw many of the Pharisees and Sadducees coming for baptism, he said to them, "You brood of vipers, who warned you to flee from the wrath to come? Therefore bear fruit in keeping with repentance;"*[83]

That's weird. That's salvation based on what we do, not based on faith alone. Huh.

Oh, I see, in this passage John is talking to the Pharisees before Jesus' ministry. So he's only talking about what a person must do before Jesus came onto the scene.

Let me find the next place in the Bible where the method of salvation is discussed.

> *Jesus said, "For I say to you that unless your righteousness surpasses that of the scribes and Pharisees, you will not enter the kingdom of heaven."*[84]

Well, there goes my 'Pharisees only' idea. In Jesus' first recorded statement on salvation, he told his own converts that they needed to be more righteous than the Pharisees if they want to go to the Kingdom of Heaven. I don't know why he didn't first tell them that righteousness comes by faith; it must have been really hard for those people to know that.

Let me find the next place in the Bible where the method of salvation is discussed.

> *You have heard that it was said, "YOU SHALL LOVE YOUR NEIGHBOR and hate your enemy." But I say to you, love your enemies and pray for those who persecute you, so that you may be sons of your Father who is in heaven;*[85]

Boy, convincing Maria is going to be harder than I thought. I finally found the very first verse in the New Testament about who is a 'son of God' and who is not. But the verse says that those who love their enemies are the sons of God.

Wow. Now, I can see why it's very hard for Maria to see

---

83 Matthew 3:7-8 NASB
84 Matthew 5:20 NASB
85 Matthew 5:43-45 NASB

that salvation is about faith. Passages like this must really confuse her. Hopefully, the next place in the Bible where the method of salvation is taught will be easier for Maria to understand.

'Forgive us our debts, as we also have forgiven our debtors.'[86]

I thought it was going to be easy to make my list! But the verse above is one of the most important verses in all the New Testament. In all the New Testament, Jesus only taught us to pray in one way, and these words are in that prayer: 'forgive us our debts, as we also have forgiven our debtors.'

How strange that in the only prayer Jesus taught, we are told to ask God to forgive our sins only in proportion to the amount that we have forgiven others.

Let me set this aside. I gotta keep making the list. Besides, I know that because we are saved by faith, I shouldn't take this literally anyway. Let me find the next Biblical entry discussing the method of salvation.

Because if you forgive others for their transgressions then your heavenly Father will also forgive you. But if you do not forgive others, then your Father will not forgive your transgressions.[87]

Sometimes, I have to wonder if Jesus knew the impact his words would have on the world. He makes it sound like it's literally true that we can only be forgiven to the degree we forgive others. Doesn't he realize that passages like this make it sound as if our salvation depends on our response to other people? Doesn't he understand that when he says these kinds of things, it confuses people like Maria? And doesn't he understand how hard he makes it for me to make my list? (lol)

Anyway, let me plug away. Let me find the next Biblical entry that deals with the method of salvation.

Do not judge so that you will not be judged. For in the way you judge, you will be judged; and by your standard of measure, it will be measured to you.[88]

---

86   Matthew 6:12 NASB
87   Matthew 6:14-15 NASB
88   Matthew 7:2 NASB

This isn't funny anymore. Jesus once again makes it sound like our judgment will be based on the way we've judged other people.

I've only just begun making my list and I already have three places where Jesus says our salvation depends on what we do to other people. Why does he say this three times over: once in the prayer we're taught to pray, once after the prayer, and now in this passage too? Why is he repeating this over and over again? Now I'm the one starting to get a little confused.

Hopefully, the next Biblical entry on the method of salvation will clear everything up.

> In everything, therefore, treat people the same way you want them to treat you, for this is the Law and the Prophets. Enter through the narrow gate; for the gate is wide and the way is broad that leads to destruction, and there are many who enter through it. For the gate is small and the way is narrow that leads to life, and there are few who find it.[89]

Instead of clearing everything up, this has got to be the most difficult passage I've ever read so far. Jesus says the Golden Rule is the way to life, and then he immediately gives six stories about Judgment Day. Since the topic is 'following the Golden Rule', then these judgment stories are about the fate of those who follow the Golden Rule and the fate of those who don't. But this can't be. There has to be something wrong.

Now my list contains four places where Jesus taught that our salvation depends on how we treat other people: Jesus taught us to ask God only to forgive our sins to the degree we've forgiven others their sins; Jesus taught that our sins are only forgiven if we forgive other people their sins; he taught that we will not be judged only if we don't judge other people; and now he openly teaches that treating other people the way we want to be treated is the narrow road that leads to life and he even adds a bunch of parables about Judgment Day to boot. What the heck is going on here?

Please, God, please allow the next Biblical entry to make everything clear.

---

89   Matthew 7:12-14 NASB

Therefore, everyone who confesses Me before men, I will also confess him before My Father who is in heaven. But whoever denies Me before men, I will also deny him before My Father who is in heaven.[90]

Praise you, God! I'm finally at one of the statements that my church says teaches salvation by faith! Here's a passage I can use. I've heard these verses many, many times in my church. Let me keep reading.

Therefore, everyone who confesses Me before men, I will also confess him before My Father who is in heaven. But whoever denies Me before men, I will also deny him before My Father who is in heaven. Do not think that I came to bring peace on the earth; I did not come to bring peace, but a sword. "For I came to SET A MAN AGAINST HIS FATHER, AND A DAUGHTER AGAINST HER MOTHER, AND A DAUGHTER-IN-LAW AGAINST HER MOTHER-IN-LAW; and A MAN'S ENEMIES WILL BE THE MEMBERS OF HIS HOUSEHOLD. He who loves father or mother more than Me is not worthy of Me; and he who loves son or daughter more than Me is not worthy of Me. And he who does not take his cross and follow after Me is not worthy of Me. He who has found his life will lose it, and he who has lost his life for My sake will find it.[91]

That's it. Now I'm more confused than ever. I had been taught that the first two sentences prove salvation by faith, yet these sentences are a part of one of the strongest passages demanding total commitment that I've ever read in the Bible. I've been taught to think about these two sentences in a way that contradicts the larger message Jesus was delivering: we have to lose our life (give up our entire life) and follow him. There's no way I can justify 'salvation by faith alone' when I read the words inside the whole passage. In the passage, the type of 'confessing' involves 'taking up our cross' and 'losing our life to find it'. This isn't the type of confessing I was taught — acknowledging Jesus is Lord with my lips and thereby receiving him as my personal savior.

Dear God, what is happening? I was told the verses teach salvation by faith, but they are found in a passage that requires total, lifelong commitment. And every other passage in Matthew

90 Matthew 10:32-33 NASB
91 Matthew 10:32-39 NASB

prior to this also says the same thing. I can't fool myself and focus on these two sentences and pretend like the rest of the book of Matthew doesn't exist.

I'm starting to feel a little nauseous. But I'm sure my pastor knows all about these verses anyway. If I keep reading the book of Matthew, I'm sure I'll come to the salvation by faith part.

> *But I tell you that every careless word that people speak, they shall give an accounting for it in the day of judgment. For by your words you will be justified, and by your words you will be condemned."*[92]

Now it's the fifth time Jesus has said that our salvation depends on how we treat others. I'm batting '5 and 0'. Now Jesus says that on Judgment Day, we will be justified or condemned by the words we have spoken to other people.

The more I read, the more confused I get. The list of times where Jesus taught that our fate on judgment is tied to the way we treat others is getting much longer. Here I wanted to make a list of all the places Maria's church was wrong, but so far, the entire list is stacking up against me and my church. What's going on here?

> *And the enemy who sowed them is the devil, and the harvest is the end of the age; and the reapers are angels. So just as the tares are gathered up and burned with fire, so shall it be at the end of the age. The Son of Man will send forth His angels, and they will gather out of His kingdom all stumbling blocks, and those who commit lawlessness, and will throw them into the furnace of fire; in that place there will be weeping and gnashing of teeth. Then THE RIGHTEOUS WILL SHINE FORTH AS THE SUN in the kingdom of their Father. He who has ears, let him hear.*[93]

Once again, salvation by faith is hidden from the reader of Matthew. The passage says, at the end of the age, the righteous will be separated from the lawless. Since this passage is about 'the end of the age', the group of people being separated includes all of us who received the Holy Spirit by faith. Why does Jesus conceal the salvation by faith part here? Why does he make it sound like

---

92   Matthew 12:37 NASB
93   Matthew 13:39-43 NASB

even those who became Christians after the Holy Spirit came will also be judged in the same way as everyone else?

I know that the righteous are those who 'appear righteous' before God because their sins were forgiven by faith in Christ. My church has taught me this. But this is so complicated that it's going to be hard to explain to Maria. I wish the passage made things much clearer. I wish Jesus would have spoken more clearly.

Anyway, I'm not getting anywhere by going through the Bible from beginning to end. Let me see skip ahead to see if I can find a place in Matthew where Jesus clearly says that our righteousness is achieved by faith.

> But when the Son of Man comes in His glory, and all the angels with Him, then He will sit on His glorious throne. All the nations will be gathered before Him; and He will separate them from one another, as the shepherd separates the sheep from the goats; and He will put the sheep on His right, and the goats on the left.
>
> Then the King will say to those on His right, 'Come, you who are blessed of My Father, inherit the kingdom prepared for you from the foundation of the world. For I was hungry, and you gave Me something to eat; I was thirsty, and you gave Me something to drink; I was a stranger, and you invited Me in; naked, and you clothed Me; I was sick, and you visited Me; I was in prison, and you came to Me.'
>
> Then **the righteous** will answer Him, 'Lord, when did we see You hungry, and feed You, or thirsty, and give You something to drink? And when did we see You a stranger, and invite You in, or naked, and clothe You? When did we see You sick, or in prison, and come to You?'
>
> "The King will answer and say to them, 'Truly I say to you, to the extent that you did it to one of these brothers of Mine, even the least of them, you did it to Me."[94]

No. This can't be. In the book of Matthew, Jesus taught the opposite. In the book of Matthew, Jesus didn't teach that our righteousness is achieved by faith. Rather, he taught that 'righteousness' is achieved by serving the neediest of society. Jesus taught that all of humanity, including those of us who became Christians after the Holy Spirit, will be divided into two groups:

---

94 Matthew 25:31-46 NASB

those who helped the poor and those who didn't. This is just like the judgment stories Jesus taught in chapter seven: on Judgment Day, people will be divided into two groups: those who treat others the way they want to be treated and those who don't.

There simply isn't any point in adding any more passages to the list unless I can make heads or tails about what I've already written down. There has to be some connection, some common thread running throughout Jesus' statements. After all, he wouldn't teach different ways of salvation in every passage! But what is the common theme? What connects them all together?

Sunday, 10:30 PM

Got it! I really got it!

Chapters seven and twenty-five both teach that **on Judgment Day, God will treat us the same way we treated our neighbors while we were alive.** This is the principle that binds the two together.

Oh, wow! I just scanned the list of passages from Matthew that I've written and realized this principle unites them all!

On Judgment Day, God will treat us the same way we treated our neighbors while we were alive. This is why Jesus said that those who love others, including their enemies, are the sons of God.

On Judgment Day, God will treat us the same way we treated our neighbors while we were alive. This is why Jesus said that treating others the way we want to be treated is the narrow road that leads to life.

On Judgment Day, God will treat us the same way we treated our neighbors while we were alive. This is why Jesus told us to pray for our sins to be forgiven in the same way that we have forgiven the sins of others.

On Judgment Day, God will treat us the same way we treated our neighbors while we were alive. This is why Jesus said God will only forgive us if we forgive others.

On Judgment Day, God will treat us the same way we treated our neighbors while we were alive. This is why Jesus *said that if we do not judge, we will not be judged.*

On Judgment Day, God will treat us the same way we treated our neighbors while we were alive. *This is why Jesus said the words we speak to others will either condemn us or justify us on the day of judgment.*

On Judgment Day, God will treat us the same way we treated our neighbors while we were alive. *This is why Jesus said that our fate on Judgment Day depends on how much we helped the poorest of society.*

*I keep looking at the list of scriptures over and over again. And it's as plain as the big nose on my face that **this is Jesus' method of salvation**. I cannot, for the life of me, make the teachings of my church fit this list of passages of what Jesus taught. And, if I want to be totally honest about it, I have to admit that the teachings of my church actually contradict what Jesus taught in the book of Matthew. My church teaches salvation by 'faith in the atonement' while Jesus taught salvation based on a single principle: **on Judgment Day, God will treat us the same way we treated our neighbors while we were alive — nothing more, nothing less.***

In story after story, in passage after passage, it all goes back to how we treat our neighbors. Jesus taught this in so many different ways, I don't know why I never saw it before.

Oh God, what a fool I've been. This is exactly what Maria says her church teaches. And this is what Robert says he believes too! Oh God, I can see your goodness now. Thank you. Thank you. Thank you. I now see that you introduced Maria into Robert's life as an answer to my prayers, but I was too blind to see it. Praise you for guiding my son to learn Jesus' requirements for making it to heaven. And thank you for giving Robert the strength to stand up to my constant nitpicks and fights. I'm so proud of him and I can't wait to tell him in the morning.

Robert stained the last page of the journal with the tears flowing down his face. "Thank you, God. Thank you so much!"

THE END

In everything, therefore, treat people the same way you want them to treat you, for this is the Law ... Many will say to me on that day, 'Lord, Lord, did we not prophesy in Your name, and in Your name cast out demons, and in Your name perform many miracles?' And then I will declare to them, 'I never knew you; **DEPART FROM ME, YOU WHO BROKE THE LAW.**'

Matthew 7:12, 23

Appendix A

How Triangle Numbers Were Calculated

Triangle numbers were developed by Pythagoras in the sixth century BC. These numbers were so important to the Pythagoreans that they swore their oaths by triangle numbers and they even counted by them as well. So by the time Jesus was born, triangle numbers already had a seven hundred year presence in Greek culture. They had become part and parcel of everyday life.

Pythagorean triangle numbers were calculated by summing together the number itself with all the digits that preceded the number. Consider the following examples:

Triangle Number 5: Sum together 5 itself with all the digits before it (1, 2, 3, and 4). Thus, the fifth triangle number is $1 + 2 + 3 + 4 + 5 = 15$.

Triangle Number 15: Sum together 15 itself with all the digits before it (1, 2, 3, 4, 5, 6, 7, 8, 9, 10, 11, 12, 13, 14). Thus, the fifteenth triangle number is $1 + 2 + 3 + 4 + 5 + 6 + 7 + 8 + 9 + 10 + 11 + 12 + 13 + 14 + 15 = 120$.

A double triangle was the 'triangle of the triangle'. For example, 'the triangle of 5' is 15 (see above) and 'the triangle of 15' is 120 (see above); thus, 'the triangle of the triangle of 5' is 120. Hence, 120 is the double triangle of 5.

With the above examples in mind, please reconsider the following passage written in the second century by Clement of Alexandria:

> **The number 120 is a triangular number... of one triangle, namely 15... From the unity of the triangles, the fifth becomes 15.**[95]

As you can see, the Pythagorean triangle numbers enjoyed popularity in early Greek writings, including the writings of the earliest

---

95   Clement of Alexandria, *The Stromata*, Book VI, excerpted from paragraphs 4 and 5.

Church fathers as well. Excavations of Pompeii revealed triangle numbers were so popular that the lower socio-economic graffiti artists were even intimately familiar with them. Furthermore, the excavation in Pompeii also showed that *triangle numbers were associated with 'the numbers of people's names'*.[96] This was a critical finding. For we now know that when the first century people read 'the number of the beast's name is 666', they would have instantly recognized that the Beast was 'an eighth'.[97]

---

96   "Harmonia, the number of her honorable name is 45." — Inscription found in Pompeii.
97   For 666 belongs to the eighth triangular unit. 666 is the 'triangle of the triangle' of eight, just as 120 is the 'triangle of the triangle' of 5.

The Jesus Secret

The men who first translated the Bible directly from Koine Greek into English didn't know the Koine language ever even existed. Therefore they translated the Bible based on Classical Greek defintions, using meanings of words that were four hundred years out of date. The end result was a rewrite of the entire text instead of an actual translation.

The Jesus Secret by Michael Wood documents what the original Koine passages actually taught. *The Jesus Secret* reveals biblical teachings that had been buried for almost two thousand years.

The Jesus Secret is now available at Amazon.com and other book retailers.

The Jerome Conspiracy

At the beginning of the Christian faith the Orthodox teaching was temporary punishment in the afterlife. The teaching of eternal punishment became the mainstream view in the fifth century when changes were made to the Bible itself. *The Jerome Conspiracy* by Michael Wood documents the previously unwritten history of how the teaching of hell became part of the Christian faith and Bible.

The Jerome Conspiracy is now available at Amazon.com and other book retailers.

For more information on The Unhidden Bible book series please visit:

www.TheUnhiddenBible.org

For more information on books published by Tubi Publication, LLC or to submit a manuscript for consideration please visit:

www.TubiPublishing.com

CPSIA information can be obtained at www.ICGtesting.com
Printed in the USA
LVOW081158130613

338408LV00001B/263/P